O9-AIC-448

ENCOURAGEMENT

The Key to Caring

Zondervan books by Lawrence J. Crabb, Jr. . . .

Basic Principles of Biblical Counseling
Effective Biblical Counseling
The Marriage Builder: A Blueprint for Counselors and Couples
Encouragement: The Key to Caring
Understanding People

ENCOURAGEMENT

The Key to Caring

Lawrence J. Crabb, Jr.
and
Dan B. Allender

PYRANEE BOOKS

Zondervan Publishing House
Grand Rapids, Michigan

Encouragement: The Key to Caring

This is a Pyranee Book
Published by the Zondervan Publishing House
1415 Lake Drive, S.E., Grand Rapids, Michigan 49506

Copyright © 1984 by The Zondervan Corporation
Grand Rapids, Michigan

Library of Congress Cataloging in Publication Data
Crabb, Lawrence J.
Encouragement: the key to caring.
1. Encouragement—Religious aspects—Christianity.
I. Allender, Dan B. II. Title.
BV4647.E53C73 1984   248.4   84-3526
ISBN 0-310-22590-6

Unless otherwise indicated, Scripture quotations are from the *New American Standard Bible*, copyright © 1960, 1962, 1963, 1968, 1971, 1972 by the Lockman Foundation, La Habra, California.

All rights reserved. No part of this publication may be reproduced, stored in a retrieval system, or transmitted in any form or by any means— electronic, mechanical, photocopy, recording, or any other—except for brief quotations in printed reviews, without the prior permission of the publisher.

In some instances, masculine pronouns are used generically.

Edited by Lisa Garvelink and James E. Ruark
Designed by Louise Bauer and James E. Ruark

Printed in the United States of America

88 89 90 91 92 / AF / 12 11 10 9 8

To our wives,
Rachael and Rebecca,
who know how to deeply
encourage their husbands

Contents

Preface 9

Chapter 1. Introduction 11

PART I. UNDERSTANDING ENCOURAGEMENT

Chapter 2. The Power of a Well-Timed Word 19

Chapter 3. Surface Community: The Obstacle to
Encouragement 27

Chapter 4. Total Openness: The Wrong Solution 39

Chapter 5. Total Commitment: The Right Solution .. 47

Chapter 6. The Character of an Encourager 55

Chapter 7. When Do We Tell Somebody Else How
We Feel? 61

PART II. THE PROCESS OF ENCOURAGEMENT

Chapter 8. How Encouragement Works 71

Chapter 9. Encouragement: The Context for Change . 83

Chapter 10. Opportunities for Encouragement 93

Chapter 11. Responding to Opportunities 103

Chapter 12. Techniques of Encouragement: I 111

Chapter 13. Techniques of Encouragement: II 121

Chapter 14. The Local Church: A Restoring
Community 131

Preface

Encouragement is important business. It merits our careful attention, not only because Scripture tells us directly to think about it, but also because it represents the unique value of Christian fellowship. Any group of compatible people can enjoy themselves, but Christians can enrich their social enjoyment with the knowledge that when they spend time together, they can have an eternally significant impact on one another.

The Book of Hebrews tells us to "encourage one another." After reviewing the unique privileges that belong to us because of Christ's past work as sin-bearer and His present work as priest, the writer to the Hebrews (10:19–25) urges us to think about three things. First, we are to approach God with a conscious awareness of our absolute acceptance in Christ. Second, because God is faithful, we are to cling tenaciously to the prospect of our eternal acceptance in heaven. Third, we are to give serious thought to how we can encourage one another.

We are reminded in Hebrews 3:12–14 that difficulties along the path of obedience can weaken our determination to follow Christ—and therefore we should encourage one another. The thought in both Scripture passages seems to be that we are to motivate each other to walk with the Lord more closely, "encouraging" one another to live out the truth of our position in Christ by loving others and doing good works.

This book is an effort to obey the invitation to "consider how to stimulate one another to love and good deeds, not forsaking our own assembling together . . . but encouraging one another; and all the more, as you see the day drawing near" (Heb. 10:24–25).

In earlier books, I have sought to show that the work of counseling belongs in the church. Local churches can and should assume responsibility for restoring troubled people to lives of effective worship and service. It is gratifying to see that more and more churches are recognizing this responsibility and are making efforts to include counseling among their ministries. In developing a counseling ministry, churches must give prime attention to helping their people become encouragers. The first step toward making counseling in the local church a reality is to train every committed church member in the skills of counseling by encouragement.

A simply worded definition of encouragement might be this: *Encouragement is the kind of expression that helps someone want to be a better Christian, even when life is rough.* By the grace of God, I can have that effect on your life and you can have it on mine. We must apply our mental energies to the job of understanding precisely how we can perform this important work for each other.

1

Introduction

The more I understand people and their needs, the more I am persuaded that God has uniquely designed the local church to respond to those needs. And as my conviction grows, so does my frustration.

The needs of people, to at least some degree, are obvious to all but the most insensitive and self-centered. Even a casual consideration of the healing potential of relationship with Christ makes it clear that the deep wounds of hurting people can be substantially healed. But still we attend to lesser matters and lose sight of what can be done. The church, where Christ's holiness and love are to be evidenced the most, too often becomes an organization just seeking to perpetuate itself, while the reasons why it should continue and grow are obscured.

When the central dynamic of living in relationship with God and each other is made secondary to concern for better facilities, expanded programs, or more staff, then the quietly enriching and soul-stirring excitement of life in Christ is numbed. The Christian life is in danger of being reduced to (depending on the personality of the leadership) either a pep rally for Jesus or an irritating set of restrictions.

The muscles of relationship within the Christian body atrophy when we fail to exercise them, and the church becomes limp. Attendance falls off, volunteers to teach Sunday school and serve on the missions committee are hard to come by, and a vague but strong mood of indifference spreads through the body. Rather than realizing that the life of the church lies in its worshipful relationship to God and its loving fellowship with one another, the leadership may diagnose the problems as weak commitment, boring services, or rebellious attitudes. These problems may indeed exist and require remedy, but they might not be the core issue.

The church often responds to such misdiagnoses by trying to create and maintain a soul-grabbing level of excitement and by legislating stronger commitment for members who fail to catch the disease of induced enthusiasm. Church services may begin reflecting a polished professionalism more appropriate to a black-tie-and-tails banquet than to a meeting of the family. Stragglers from the fold may be called back with noisy exhortations that give the impression that church life is one long boot camp directed by a tough drill sergeant. Through it all, the potential of the church for satisfying longings and for nourishing life diminishes. Worship becomes ritual, and teaching loses power.

How can we recapture our focus in the church? What can we do to shift our attention back to relating to God and to each other in loving fellowship and mutual ministry? The task is especially difficult because each of us tends to regard our focus as clear and the other person's as blurred. No pastor would say that his church does *not* revolve around loving God and loving others.

One pastor will argue—I think correctly—that his emphasis on expository preaching directs attention to God's character and people's problems by presenting biblical truth. Another will maintain that his body-life church is more on target. Still another will speak warmly of the possibility of reaching more people with God's love through expanded facilities and will thus regard his building program as consistent with the church's purpose for being.

Church life seems to pass through various stages. The era of tent revivals and sawdust-trail conversions has largely yielded to a more settled (and stifling?) approach to doing the work of the church. In some circles, the emotionalism of rededication invitations has been replaced with a more sober emphasis on meaty teaching. But for some, that kind of teaching seems to result in cold orthodoxy.[1] So they strive to inject new life into the ecclesiastical corpses through innovations such as sharing groups. These groups attempt to strip away masks of phony contentment and to uncover the gutsy problems raging inside people. The idea is

---

[1]If Bible teaching produces cold orthodoxy, then it's very likely that the teaching is merely academic exercise rather than the dynamic presentation of truth.

to build relationships through self-disclosure followed by mutual affirmation.

Critical observers have noted, however, that a relational focus can shift the foundation of the church away from "dry" truth to vibrant experience. The Bible may then become less the *authority* for belief and behavior and more the *stimulus* for fervent fellowship. Meetings for Bible study to which participants come armed with commentaries and concordances have sometimes given way to prayer-and-share groups to which people bring their needs, experiences, and opinions—and occasionally an unstudied Bible. *Sharing* one's faith may then become more important than *knowing* one's faith.

Fellowships that attend more to relationships than to the truths upon which relationships can be built run serious risks. Divisions, superficiality, and a shift in authority from God's Word to human experience argue for a different focus. But what?

Every alternative has its own disclaimer. Old-fashioned revivalism, for some, is culturally outdated; expository preaching may seem to sail harmlessly over the heads of the shallow masses; a body-life emphasis puts people uncomfortably close to each other where tensions surface and squabbles may break out. The answer for many has been the Big Church: culturally in vogue, appealing to the success-conditioned masses, offering opportunity to be lost in the crowd or involved in a group—whichever your taste may be.

Church growth experts (who usually define growth in numerical terms) help local leaders to polish their promotional skills and refine their community appeal. Using organizational strategies developed and tested by industry, they have transformed struggling church fellowships into prosperous business enterprises—an achievement of dubious value. Think big and you'll get big.

And what argument can be raised against bigness? Who can voice objection to increased attendance without inviting scorn for lack of vision and evangelistic concern? *Diversified programs* to reach all special-interest groups (singles, older folks, young marrieds, the mission-minded), *improved musical performances* (and I'm all for asking the off-key soprano to reevaluate her gifts), and *more relevant and practical preaching* (which makes the Sunday morning sermon the inspirational and socially chic hub of church life) are a few characteristics of the big church.

Watching these developments are numbers of small fellowships in simple buildings who fervently cling to a well-defined set of unique convictions, adamantly refusing to be caught up in the latest church fad. But too often, as these sincere Christians continue on faithfully, their convictions harden into complacency, and doctrinal orthodoxy declines into dogmatic traditionalism. Because the right way is narrow and often missed, lack of growth and outreach may be unconsciously but proudly regarded as testimony to ecclesiological purity.

A FOCUS ON PEOPLE

What are we to do? I have my ideas, and you have yours. Some of us want to return to evangelistic campaigns; others place a high premium on exegetical teaching that gets us beyond milk and into meat; some see the answer in body-life fellowships with a relational focus; and still others dream of big churches with the confidence that a Big God can do Big Things.

In whatever direction we move, one thing is clear. Church life involves people getting together, people in contact with other people—whether in small groups or huge sanctuaries, whether in praise meetings or teaching classes, whether in evangelistic campaigns or worship services. When any emphasis in our church life interferes at all with our effort to *better understand the resources of Christ and to more effectively minister to needy people*, then the church has lost its way. The church is people—God's people.

Exegetical teaching, soul-winning visitation, small-group fellowships, fund-raising campaigns, and choir rehearsals all have a legitimate—and even essential—function in the church's central purpose. But if these or other activities are not consciously and continuously regarded as means for drawing us closer to God and making disciples of all men, then we are draining our churches of their energizing core.

Our churches can be like the wealthy man whose family starves to death emotionally while he is working hard to better provide for them materially. They can feverishly continue with the appearance of success while many of their members struggle to hold their lives together. How sad! People are troubled and restless and angry and desperate and empty and worried. They need to know God and to learn what it means to live in relationship with Him and with His people. Our churches have untapped resources for responding to that need.

We must not go on with business as usual. Local churches have the responsibility to restore troubled people to peaceful, purposeful lives that can then bear testimony to God's redeeming power before a watching world.

Continue with evangelistic efforts, strengthen the teaching ministry, provide more opportunities for fellowship, build appropriate facilities, expand church programs, honor convictions—but in all that is done, keep two pivotal truths clearly in mind:

1. *People are hurting more deeply than we know* (and more than they themselves sometimes know, like the person who is not yet aware that cancer has formed in his body);
2. *Relationship with Christ provides resources unique and indispensable to substantially heal now and perfectly heal forever.*

This book is about a core element in church life that derives its importance from these two facts. Every church, whatever its distinctive emphasis, needs this element; its presence creates the atmosphere for knowing Christ in life-changing ways, and its absence leaves the atmosphere too overcast for the glory of God to shine through. This book is about Encouragement.

Every Christian, regardless of gift or training, is called upon to encourage his brothers and sisters. Whatever the direction in which our particular congregation is moving, church life will include spending time in the presence of other Christians. And when we meet together as God's people, we are to encourage one another, to say and do things that stimulate others to a deeper appreciation of Christ and to stronger commitment to our relationship with Him and with each other.

All Bible-believing churches in which the redeeming love of Christ is faithfully proclaimed should be known for their emphasis on encouragement.

What does it mean to encourage one another? How does encouragement work? Is it really that important? What is its effect? What must be true of my life before I can encourage someone else? How does encouragement fit into the life of the church? How is encouragement distinct from everyday kindness? Can encouragement really penetrate deeply into someone's life rather than merely provide a temporary lift? This book addresses these questions.

Part 1
UNDERSTANDING
ENCOURAGEMENT

2
The Power of a Well-Timed Word

When Sigmund Freud discovered that symptoms of emotional distress could sometimes be relieved simply by talking in certain ways to his patients, he was puzzled and intrigued. Years of medical training had conditioned him to think of people as merely biological and chemical entities. He had concluded that problems like anxiety, depression, or phobias must reflect some physical disorder treatable only through medical intervention.

Had Freud spent time studying the Book of Proverbs, perhaps he would have been less surprised to discover that mere words can have such strong impact. Listen to what the inspired writer says about the power of words:

Death and life are in the power of the tongue (Prov. 18:21);

Good words can make an anxious heart glad (Prov. 12:25);

A soothing tongue is a tree of life (Prov. 15:4);

Pleasant words are . . . sweet to the soul and healing to the bones (Prov. 16:24);

Like apples of gold in settings of silver
Is a word spoken in right circumstances (Prov. 25:11).

The Scriptures also say that speaking light words of cheer at the wrong time is "like one who takes off a garment on a cold day" (Prov. 25:20).

Words are important. They have very real power. James warns us that although the tongue is a small part of the body, it has the power to determine the whole course of human existence (James 3:5–6).

When God instructs us to encourage one another whenever we come together, He is including the admonition to harness the power of words for a specific purpose. Of course, there are many ways to encourage one another by kind deeds as well as by kind words—taking food to sick friends, visiting folks in the hospital or inviting new folks in church to dinner. But the capacity of words to do serious damage or great good makes *verbal* encouragement an especially important topic to consider. And that is the theme of this book: *encouragement through the careful selection of words that are intended to influence another person meaningfully toward increased godliness.*

The key passage in Hebrews which instructs us to encourage one another uses a word for encouragement that means literally "to stir up, to provoke, to incite people in a given direction." Verbal encouragement includes the idea of one person's joining someone else on a journey and speaking words that encourage the traveler to keep pressing on despite obstacles and fatigue.

I can recall standing by the finish line at many track meets, waiting for my son to come straining down the last stretch of a two-mile run. Exhausted by the labor of pushing himself to his limit and sometimes bothered by a variety of aches and cramps, he was sorely tempted to collapse fifty yards short of the finish line.

As each of our team's runners came into view, the line of paunchy, out-of-shape fathers would take up the cry, "C'mon, only a few yards to go! Push! Push! Kick up your legs! You can do it!" And most of the young athletes would respond to these words by grimacing with determination, narrowing their eyes, and pumping their legs with renewed strength until they crossed the line.

I have never yet heard a father call out to his son during that final stretch, "You look tired! Why don't you quit? You're in the back third of the field anyway. Maybe running isn't your sport." Yet I have overheard a Christian say to a young man after he had taught his first Sunday school class, "When is the regular teacher coming back?" There really isn't much difference between the words.

Some parents at track meets have stood quietly in a visible place while their sons puffed by. In more than one instance the boy has looked over, caught a quick glimpse of his beaming parent, and then picked up the pace. Sometimes the power of words depends upon timing. A comment like "You looked great!" was reserved for that special moment when mother and dad handed a welcome glass of cold water to their parched, grateful son. "How delightful is a timely word" (Prov. 25:23).

SHALLOW WORDS

Many people seem to live in utter disregard of the effect of their words on others. A visitor from another culture once related to me the nearly crushing disappointment he experienced during his first few months in a North American church.

After an evening fellowship-type service in which he had been warmly introduced to the body, a number of people went out of their way to greet him. Several added to their welcome an implied invitation: "We'd love to have you over for dinner sometime soon." The young man was delighted. He spent the next week eagerly waiting for the phone to ring, sometimes rushing home from work in order not to miss the call he knew would come. It did not come—not until three months later. He told me that to adjust to American culture, he had to learn that many words were spoken without meaning.

Many of our polite greetings—"Good to see you" or "Let's get together sometime" or "How are you? I haven't talked to you in ages!"—are gracefully disguised ways of saying, "Keep your distance; I'm just being polite." It is interesting—and more than a bit distressing—to notice how often our social and business interactions say one thing and mean quite another.

I never fail to feel somewhat awkward as I file by the flight attendants after an airplane trip. I sense an obligation to make brief eye contact and smile quickly when they look at me, grin, and say, "Good to have you on board." The whole exchange seems dreadfully insincere.

I usually make very few demands on a stewardess when I fly. A reading light that works and nonsmokers who don't smoke are all that I require. Perhaps as I walk by, the words "Good to have you on board" come honestly.

But when the *bon vivant,* who without solicitation assumes the role of social director during the flight and demands immediate and frequent refills of his cocktail glass, staggers through the exit, I wonder if the tight smile and the words "Good to have you on board" might really mean something else.

I suppose we must accept that everyday life will include many situations where words are less meant than appropriate. But it should not be that way in the church. How often, I wonder, is fellowship among Christians characterized by no more depth than flight attendants bidding farewell to disembarking passengers? Do our conversations often consist of the exchange of empty words that only seem to convey a message of concern and love?

There is nothing wrong, of course, with social chitchat or polite friendliness in their place. I am certainly not proposing that every word we utter be draped in priestly vestments and spoken in organ tones. The issue is not between heavy words versus light words. It rather involves *sincere* versus *insincere* words or perhaps between *consistently shallow* versus *meaningful* words. Everything is wrong with insincere and predictably shallow words. They encourage no one.

The prophet Jeremiah indicted the religious leaders of his day for healing the wounds of God's people superficially (Jer. 6:14). A physician who diagnosed a potentially fatal condition that surgery could cure and who then prescribed lots of liquid and two aspirin a day would be guilty of malpractice. The priests of Israel did precisely that in spiritual matters. They recommended cheerful optimism in the face of impending judgment for sin.

We often do the same sort of thing. It is far too easy for churches to provide surface healing, a shallow lift that lasts until the benediction. But to effect temporary relief from pain through words that fail to touch the real disease and then to refer stubborn cases that don't improve to counseling resources outside the church is nothing less than spiritual malpractice. Local Bible-believing churches consist of people who know Christ and who therefore have the power to influence others deeply through the careful use of words. The words of Christians reflect, in some measure at least, the reality of Christ's love and sufficiency in their lives.

Yet we settle for shallow words. "Good to have you here," we glibly say as people file out of the sanctuary. Comments that appear to be friendly and helpful but fail to recognize the power of words to affect people have little place in the life of a healthy church. Shallow words do not encourage.

DEATH WORDS

Once we see that words can have power, we must no longer be content with shallow words that mean little. We must set out to harness that power with a clear awareness that words can both tear down and build up. They are much like a sharp knife that in the hands of a surgeon can heal, but in the hands of a careless child can kill. "Death and life are in the power of the tongue" (Prov. 28:21).

Consider how words can destroy. A middle-aged man had been struggling for years with chronic depression. Several psychiatrists had agreed that the root problem was chemical and that maintenance dosages of antidepressant drugs would be required for the rest of his life.

In the course of our counseling, the man related to me that his father, the self-made head of a large corporation, had repeatedly told him, "Son, when you inherit the family business, I expect that you will ruin it."

These words stung more painfully each time he heard them When his father died, the man felt driven to work unreasonably long hours to prove his prediction wrong. The pressure to avoid failure that relentlessly gnawed at him was quieted only by alcohol. Soon a serious drinking problem developed. His wife threatened to leave him. Finally he succumbed to ongoing depression for which he could find relief only in drugs. His life was devastated by the power of his father's tongue.

I was once teaching a large Sunday school class when a particularly conscientious young man asked a question. My mind quickly came up with a comical reply, though I don't know why. I put the thought into words and won a laugh. Six months later the young man came to me to resolve the bitterness triggered by that incident, in which he had felt terribly embarrassed. It might be argued that the man was overly sensitive. But the point remains that words were the instruments of damage.

LIFE WORDS

The bright side of the picture is that words can not only sting, but soothe. Far more important, they can even reroute a life from a bad direction to a good one. These are the words—words of life and encouragement—with which I am concerned.

The apostle Paul instructs us in Ephesians 4:29 to ". . . let no unwholesome word proceed from your mouth, but only such a word as is good for edification according to the need of the moment, that it may give grace to those who hear." One illustration demonstrates how a few well-timed words suited perfectly to the need of a particular moment yielded enduring results in my life.

As a youngster I developed a thoroughly annoying and humiliating problem of stuttering. Any person afflicted with this puzzling menace can tell you that certain letters and sounds are especially hard to say. Two troublesome letters for me were *L* and *P*. My name is *Larry* and I attended *Plymouth*-Whitemarsh junior and senior high schools in Pennsylvania.

In the ninth grade, I was elected president of our junior high student body. During an assembly of the seventh, eighth, and ninth grades—several hundred students—I was beckoned by the principal to join him on stage for the induction ceremony.

Standing nervously in front of the squirming, bored crowd, I was told to repeat after the principal the words, "I, Larry Crabb of Plymouth-Whitemarsh Junior High School, do hereby promise . . ." That's how the principal said it. My version was a bit different: "I, L-L-L-L-Larry Crabb of P-P-P-P-Plymouth-Whitemarsh Junior High School, do hereby p-p-p-promise . . ."

The principal was sympathetically perplexed, my favorite English teacher wanted to cry, a few students laughed out loud, most were awkwardly amused, some felt bad for me—and I died a thousand deaths. I decided right then that public speaking was not for me.

A short time later, our church celebrated the Lord's supper in a Sunday morning worship service. It was customary in our congregation to encourage young men to enter into the privilege of worship by standing and praying aloud. That particular Sunday I sensed the pressure of the saints (not, I fear, the leading of the Spirit), and I responded by unsteadily leaving my chair, for the first time, with the intention of praying.

Filled less with worship than with nervousness, I found my theology becoming confused to the point of heresy. I remember thanking the Father for hanging on the cross and praising Christ for triumphantly bringing the Spirit from the grave. Stuttering throughout, I finally thought of the word *Amen* (perhaps the first evidence of the Spirit's leading), said it, and sat down. I recall staring at the floor, too embarrassed to look around, and solemnly vowing *never again* to pray or speak aloud in front of a group. Two strikes were enough.

When the service was over, I darted toward the door, not wishing to encounter an elder who might feel obliged to correct my twisted theology. But I was not quick enough. An older Christian man named Jim Dunbar intercepted me, put his arm on my shoulder, and cleared his throat to speak.

I remember thinking to myself, "Here it comes. Oh well, just endure it and then get to the car." I then listened to this godly gentleman speak words that I can repeat verbatim today, more than twenty years later.

"Larry," he said, "there's one thing I want you to know. Whatever you do for the Lord, I'm behind you one thousand percent." Then he walked away.

Even as I write these words, my eyes fill with tears. I have yet to tell that story to an audience without at least mildly choking. Those words were life words. They had power. They reached deep into my being. My resolve never again to speak publicly weakened instantly.

Since the day those words were spoken, God has led me into a ministry in which I regularly address and pray before crowds of all sizes. I do it without stuttering. I love it. Not only death, but also life lies in the power of the tongue.

God intends that we be people who use words to encourage one another. A well-timed word has the power to urge a runner to finish the race, to rekindle hope when despair has set in, to spark a bit of warmth in an otherwise cold life, to trigger healthful self-evaluation in someone who doesn't think much about his shortcomings, to renew confidence when problems have the upper hand.

SUMMARY

Christians are commanded to encourage one another. Because words have the power to affect people deeply, it is appropriate to consider how to encourage fellow Christians through what we say.

Words can encourage, discourage, or do nothing. Shallow words accomplish little, death words discourage, and life words encourage. We must learn to speak sincerely with positive impact, using our words to help other Christians pursue the pathway of obedience more zealously.

3
Surface Community: The Obstacle to Encouragement

W hen we gather together at church dinners or in small groups or mingle in the parking lot after the Sunday morning service, the sentences we speak often do little more than shift about the social currents. Few people have a sense that their words make much difference to anyone else. Why do our words lack power? Do our words really matter? How do we typically use them?

Observe two people in conversation. You will most likely notice that the speaker is looking at the listener, but the listener is not looking at the speaker. The reason is obvious: *the listener is not listening.* He is waiting till the speaker pauses so that he can regain the floor. Neither asks the other questions of consequence. The dialogue is more like two monologues, each without an audience. Sometimes one party is especially dominant and the other patient or passive.

I was flying to Chicago as I wrote this chapter. Behind me sat a man who, judging by the loud conversation I had no choice but to hear, is an authority on everything. For an hour his topics ranged from the best price on floor tiles to finding good help in the restaurant business to the quality of nursing care in Florida's hospitals—and the man had yet to admit ignorance or even a hint of uncertainty about anything.

I suspect that the bored but gracious and patient victim sitting in the adjoining seat—a pleasant-looking, middle-aged woman— could suggest questions about nuclear physics, the Arab-Israeli conflict, or medieval religious practices and hear a learned discourse spoken as by an expert and interrupted by very few pauses. As near as I could tell, the conversation was utterly pointless, unless the woman will "count it all joy" to learn patience amid trials. The interaction was a lopsided exchange of worthless words that gave evidence of serving no useful purpose.

Too many times, our words display no more value than that airborne conversation. We throw them about the way a toddler might carelessly play with a hundred-dollar bill. Yet, when our Lord Jesus taught, the people immediately perceived that He spoke with authority. His words had power. They were somehow different from the endless flow of words that came from the Pharisees in His audience.

What prevents our words from having power? How do we bridge the distance between us and others so that what we say bears weight? Offering an answer requires that we first understand the problem of *surface community*, a kind of relational structure that prevents words from realizing their potential to encourage.

THE CORE OF PEOPLE

People make up communities, and it is also people who erect barriers to meaningful interaction. To understand how barriers are built and how we can remove them, we must first ask why we create hindrances that block our words from reaching others and prevent the closeness we desire. A true perspective on the matter requires that we examine the first historical instance of these barriers. The story is related in the third chapter of the Book of Genesis.

Before he sinned, Adam enjoyed unclouded fellowship with God. There were no walls, no distance, no tension. But sin immediately brought terrible consequences. Among them was the presence of a new emotion: fear.

In response to this new emotion, Adam fled from God and went into hiding. Obviously, an all-seeing God knew that Adam was fearfully crouching behind the tree. But He called out to Adam and asked a question—the first question asked of sinful man by a holy God: "Adam, where are you?" Perhaps God wanted to create in Adam a realization of his plight and to provoke a confession of sin. Only *exposed* problems motivate people to ask for help.

Note Adam's response: "I was afraid because I was naked; so I hid myself" (Gen. 3:10). His answer separates naturally into three distinct parts:

1. *I was afraid:* Adam's core emotion;

2. *Because I was naked:* his core motivation;
3. *So I hid myself:* his core strategy.

THE CORE EMOTION

Consider Adam's core emotion. He was afraid. Before he sinned, there was nothing to fear. He was on friendly terms with God, he knew nothing of marital squabbles, the food supply was plentiful in a garden with no weeds, and his job was both secure and meaningful.

But when sin entered paradise, paradise was lost. Disorder, uncertainty, emotional stress, broken relationships, and death were introduced. Life's perplexing questions suddenly confronted him, as they have his descendants ever since: Is there a solution? Will life work? Am I doomed to eternal rejection? Can I make it on my own? Will my marriage fail? And what is the common element in these questions? All were prompted by fear.

Throughout Scripture, God repeatedly deals with the problem of fear. When Abraham was concerned about his future, God said, "Do not fear, Abram, I am a shield to you" (Gen. 15:1). When Jeremiah was called by God to preach to a rebellious nation, the prophet quickly declined the invitation. Rather than rebuking Jeremiah for his stubborn defiance, however, God struck at the heart of the matter when He said, "Do not be afraid of them, for I am with you to deliver you" (Jer. 1:8).

After commissioning His followers to disciple all nations—an awesome assignment—our Lord Jesus anticipated fear as the major obstacle to their obedience. He assured them, "I am with you always, even to the end of the age" (Matt. 28:20). John, the apostle of love, delighted in the truth that God's perfect love can replace fear as the controlling motive of life (1 John 4:18).

Why does the Bible place this emphasis on fear? As I contemplate the predicament of mankind and the reasons for reacting to it as we do, it seems clear to me that the governing emotional energy in the unregenerate human personality is fear. Our problems are really quite beyond our capacity to solve. We cannot control what matters most to us. The plans we make will work nicely only if factors beyond our control do not interfere. Our lives ultimately are not in our hands. So with good reason we fear what might happen.

Fear is an interesting emotion, if we distance ourselves far enough from it to view it objectively. It shows up in an incredible variety of situations as the underlying force behind what we do or experience. I do not believe strongly in the significance of dreams, but I suspect it is true that fears pushed out of our minds will occasionally surface in our dreams. Let me illustrate this.

During the past twenty-five years I have repeatedly dreamt a dream in which, though the particulars vary, the central theme remains constant. It started when I was in the eighth grade. I dreamt that I strolled into Miss Reifsnyder's math class, assumed my customary slouched position prepared to endure another hour of confusion, and leisurely opened my textbook.

I snapped to rigid attention when the teacher barked, "Clear your desks, get your number two pencils out, and get ready for your exam." Exam! What exam? In my dream I looked around frantically, hoping to see other students registering surprise. Some looked grim, but none were puzzled. I was the only student who had forgotten that this was examination day.

Throughout high school, college, and graduate school, I dreamt about similar disasters, all revolving around the theme of being unprepared for something important. Even after completing school, I remember awakening early in the morning on two or three occasions, thinking I had better study for an upcoming test. I had to shake my head a bit and remind myself that I was *giving* and no longer *taking* exams.

My dreams then shifted to a new setting—the church pulpit. I would be waiting calmly for the pastor to introduce me as the guest speaker when suddenly it hit me that I had forgotten to prepare the message. In our day, dreams rarely have prophetic significance, but this particular one came alarmingly close to literal fulfillment when I was in my early twenties.

I was preparing in real life for my first opportunity to preach at a Sunday morning service. To subdue jittery nerves, I decided to add a quotation from John Calvin to my message, reasoning that if everything else in the sermon was unhelpful and commonplace, perhaps the words of a revered theologian might redeem the sermon from total uselessness. I had recently come across Calvin's well-known line, "While it is true we are saved by faith alone, the faith that saves is never alone," so I carefully copied the words into my notes.

I dramatically set the stage when I came to the point in my sermon where I was about to repeat those impressive words. "Last week," I began, "I came across a quote that clearly ties together the truth regarding the gift of salvation and the responsibility of faith. The words so aptly express the biblical position that I have committed them to memory. They have burned themselves into my mind and I expect never to forget them. It was John Calvin who once said—" And my mind went blank. I could no more recall those words than I could recite all 176 verses of Psalm 119.

I hurriedly looked down at my notes but the pages were not in order. After shuffling through my notes—written on legal-size yellow paper and therefore hard to conceal—I finally spotted the quote and sheepishly read Calvin's unforgettable words.

When the apostle Peter preached his first sermon, three thousand souls were saved. When I delivered my first, twenty folks warmly expressed their sympathy.

Running insistently through my dreams and painfully realized at the beginning of my preaching career was the emotion of fear. It was a fear that I would not measure up to the task, that inadequate preparation would lead to unacceptable performance, that I would be exposed as less than what I want to be but what I fear I am. Adam's legacy to his children includes fear. Adam was afraid, and so are we.

THE CORE MOTIVATION

Why was Adam afraid? Responding to God's question, he pinpointed the source of his fear as nakedness: "I was afraid because I was naked." Clearly, Adam was speaking of something more than a newly developed modesty regarding physical nudity. For the first time in his life Adam had to wrestle with a sense of unacceptability. He realized that if seen in his fallen condition, if exposed as a transgressor of God's rules, he would be rejected by the ultimate Person.

If fear is the core emotion in the human personality, then the final source of our fear is an awareness of our profoundly unacceptable condition. We know something is wrong with us. We are not as we should be. Like the woman who hides her wrinkles beneath creams and make-up, we realize that we are unattractive in our undisguised condition. And if we take time to examine ourselves according to the standards of holiness—a humbling but necessary exercise—we must inevitably conclude that we are not simply unattractive, but unacceptably ugly.

It is therefore natural and legitimate to fear rejection. The fear is not neurotic, but realistic. We deserve rejection. But rejection is so terribly painful that we want above all else to avoid it. So we come to fear *exposure*, knowing almost intuitively that beneath the make-up of decency, kindness, generosity, and stylish clothing is someone who, if truly known, would provoke disapproval and criticism.

All of us, even those whose make-up is thickly applied and has been in place for years, are aware that at some level the wrinkles are there. From childhood on, as soon as we can translate our feelings into ideas, we approach life with *fear of exposure* and *fear of the rejection we predict will follow.*

Although our ultimate fear has to do with rejection by God, we learn to attach the fear to someone more tangibly present. We come to fear the rejection of parent and friend and, as we enter adulthood, spouse, children, employer, pastor, and society.

The painful experiences of life teach us whom and what to fear. A middle-aged woman related to me the hurt she had felt years earlier when the family gathered around her dying father. His wife, son, and two daughters stood near.

As he lingered for a few moments on the edge of death, the man turned to his wife of thirty years and whispered, "Honey, I've always loved you. Take care. I'll see you again." He then turned slowly to his son and struggled to say "You've been a source of real joy to me. I love you." With gasping breath he said to his older daughter, "I love you, too." And then he died.

Tears flowed as the woman told me of the rejection she felt at not hearing her father say to her, twenty-five years earlier, "I love you." Her fear of rejection ran deep. From that day on, her single goal in life was to avoid the rejection of an important man. She had come to me for counseling because her husband had just admitted to an ongoing adulterous relationship.

Each of us has undergone some sort of trauma that has aggravated our basic fear of rejection and failure. Stuttering in front of schoolmates, the divorce of one's parents, the death of a close friend, financial disaster, a teen-age daughter's pregnancy—the list goes on and on. Situations that feed fears are part of everyone's background.

Fears are like cancer cells. They intensify and multiply. Can we handle life? Does anyone really care? What would I do if. . . ? Will I make enough money? How will my kids turn out? Am I appreciated? Am I worthwhile at all, or am I what I fear—an unacceptable, unimportant, uncared-for failure?

A casual glance at the confident businessman walking easily into the exclusive restaurant or the society matron graciously welcoming expensively dressed guests into her marbled foyer might make us wonder if perhaps the "beautiful people" have overcome whatever fears they once felt. They certainly don't appear to be afraid. Perhaps the disease attacks only the struggling lower middle class or the physically unattractive or ordinary people who have no special talents or resources.

It is true that not everyone looks afraid, and many people sincerely report no *conscious experience* of fear, although a day of serious reflection might change that. *But all of us have fears.* The writer to the Hebrews speaks of the fear of death that subjects people to "slavery all their lives" (Heb. 2:15). All of us face the prospect of dying. None but the believer knows what lies on the other side of the grave. And where there is uncertainty, there is fear.

We do not know what will happen, either in life or in death. We are disturbingly aware that things may not turn out as we want, that the world may not treat us kindly. The root of our fear is an understanding, however primitive, that we are not acceptable and that exposure of who we really are will bring rejection.

If fear consumes the core of every person, how is it that we see no more evidence of it than we do? Most people sitting in church seem relaxed. Perhaps people show their fear in a doctor's waiting room, yet in most settings people seem busy, angry, cheerful, bored, excited, determined, or sad—but rarely afraid. Fellowship times in the church seem to consist of relatively happy people mingling together. Where is the fear?

THE CORE STRATEGY

"I was afraid because I was naked," Adam admitted, anticipating the cry that sinful man has uttered ever since. He was aware of his true condition, which if exposed would meet with rejection. "*So I hid.*" Adam hid in an effort to avoid dealing with what he feared. He chose fig leaves and a tree to hide behind, hoping to avoid the knowing glance that would indicate rejection. And people ever since then, following in Adam's footsteps, have been searching desperately for ways to cover their unworthiness, to feel good about themselves despite the fact that they are worthy of rejection.

Satan is most obliging. He offers dozens of strategies for

feeling good about oneself without finding acceptance in Christ. Money, fame, power, position, and luxury are among the most obvious. But equally effective are more subtle strategies: an unwillingness to examine oneself, social assertion, a critical spirit, dogmatism, shyness, sociability—whatever helps us to run from admitting who we are to anyone, including ourselves.

Fearful people committed to avoiding the terror of exposure will look for places to hide. We protect ourselves in defensive layers, much as we don heavy overcoats before venturing into a wintry blizzard.

Whenever we discover a protective strategy that works, we keep it available to put on as a layer whenever we feel the chill of developing rejection. Fear-inspired ingenuity is capable of thinking up an endless variety of protective strategies: jokes, silliness, a cocky attitude, boasting, manipulative tears, feigned repentance and humility, remaining quiet during group discussions, a drink before meeting friends, spending hours doing homework with our children, or watching television—anything that enables us to greet the world with our real selves hidden safely from sight.

Figure 1 clarifies the concept.

DEFENSIVE LAYER — *protects from exposure*

FIGURE 1

Define a *layer* as whatever we do or don't do that is intended to protect us from exposure and help us avoid whatever we fear.

People can spend their entire lives behind their layers, selecting whichever one fits the occasion, like choosing what jewelry or necktie to wear. People may refuse to talk to their spouses because previous attempts to communicate led to unfulfilling arguments. *Not talking* then becomes a layer, a defensive pattern designed to avoid a confrontation.

Some people will never offer an opinion in a Bible study because it may be ridiculed or exposed as incorrect. When this layer becomes a way of life, we might call the person "shy." Others take every opportunity to voice their ideas, thriving on being noticed. For them, *talkativeness* is a layer designed to ward off rejection by winning attention.

Many conscientious Christians do their best to hold fractured families together, struggling under peer pressure to maintain something of a homelife. Even these well-meaning and sometimes heroic efforts may be the layer of *control*, a defense against failure.

What happens when layered Christians meet together? We can picture the reality in Figure 2.

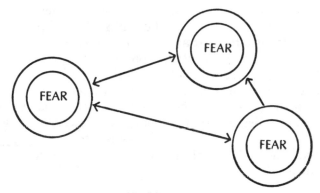

FIGURE 2

We meet at the level of our layers, determined to remain safely hidden behind our protective maneuvers. Our primary commitment is to avoid exposure, to appear acceptable, to deal from a position of strength.

When Christians interact from behind defensive masks, they experience *layer-to-layer fellowship*. This is like lovers kissing through a pane of glass. After chatting from behind our layers, we feel unsatisfied, distant, untouched, superficial—and safe.

But the cost of safety runs high. Relating from our layers

produces *surface community*, a set of shallow interchanges that can stir the inmost being no more than a pebble disturbs the ocean.

Too often, the community of layered saints compounds the problem by specifying which layers are acceptable. In some churches, members must be constantly cheerful, positive, and in a good mood. In others, a struggling humility is admired. Sometimes the right layer consists of spending a certain amount of time with God in a specified way. Sometimes it's carrying a church-sanctioned, specially embossed prayer notebook.

In these situations the fellowship becomes chained to a set of expectations that must be met if acceptance is to be granted. How wrong to specify conditions under which blood-bought saints can enjoy superior acceptance! In the apostle Paul's day, one layer was circumcision. I suspect he regards our layers much as he viewed the Judaizers' layers in Galatia (Gal. 5:1–12).

Superficiality becomes even more superficial as pressured Christians struggle to adjust their layers to local standards. Many succumb to frustration and fatigue: "I just can't measure up." Some rise to the occasion and join the ranks of the "spiritually elite." Others drift into irregular attendance, preferring the relaxation of the Sunday comics to the viselike pressure of the church.

Encouragement will not develop in surface community. A radical change from surface fellowship to meaningful encounter is needed if the church is to become a place of encouragement. The next chapter deals with the question, How can we effect the necessary change from layered fellowship to Spirit-led fellowship with God and each other? How can we replace surface community with the real thing?

SUMMARY

People are afraid of rejection. Therefore they try to avoid rejection by putting their best foot forward, that is, by wearing protective layers designed to win approval.

Our words are intended to serve the purpose of our own protection. They are self-serving. Therefore, words spoken from a layer are sinful; they do not reflect a concern for others' needs as greater than our own.

When "layered Christians" meet together, their purpose is to protect themselves from each other or to use each other to enhance their own self-esteem. Layer-to-layer fellowship produces surface community, a relational structure in which people do not really touch one another. No encouragement can take place in surface community.

We must replace surface community with biblical fellowship if we are to encourage one another when we gather together.

4
Total Openness: The Wrong Solution

Before we can learn the art of encouragement, we must first concern ourselves with creating a relational atmosphere in which words can reach deeply enough to encourage. This requires breaking down the protective walls between people that sustain surface community. Words have little chance of encouraging powerfully when spoken from one layer to another.

If layers exist to protect people from the exposure they fear, it follows that the remedy for layered fellowship primarily involves finding a solution to fear. At this point we are likely to set off in wrong directions in search of that solution.

THE DISEASE OF SHARING

On several occasions I have asked groups of people to write their answers to the question, "When or where do you feel least afraid of other people—most comfortable, relaxed, and safe?" A few have responded by listing moments when they are alone, but most described their safest times as those spent with someone they could trust to accept them. Generally we all feel most relaxed when we can let our guard down and be completely ourselves with someone who we believe will in no way reject us.

An illustration of this occurred in my home one evening. After my family had endured a head-of-the-home-type lecture on "layers," one son remarked, "I don't need to have layers when I'm around you guys because I know you love me." Comments like that do a lot to warm parental hearts. And it's true that we feel least fearful when we are with people who love us. In an atmosphere of love, we feel the freedom to be real, to shed our layers without fear of rejection. In this atmosphere, feelings of intimacy and closeness can grow naturally.

Now, begin with this idea and let it develop. Many people might reason like this:

> I want to feel comfortable and free of fear. I admit that my layers don't solve the problem of fear anymore than aspirin cures a brain tumor. They merely numb the pain. I long for a relationship in which I can strip myself of layers and expose my deepest feelings without fear of rejection. I will therefore search for a person or group with whom I can be fearlessly open.

The implications of this reasoning are clear. If we are to solve the problem of surface community and enter into layer-free relationships, we must walk through our fears by risking exposure. We need to begin opening up with others until we find someone who accepts us as we are.

Think where this search for full self-expression without rejection has led. Group therapy owes much of its popularity to the promise of openness without risk. Prostitutes make a living by guaranteeing a form of acceptance for a fee. One critic of psychotherapy described the counseling hour as the purchase of friendship. Others have referred to it as psychological prostitution: for a prepaid fee, the patient may fully reveal his bizarre fantasies and violent feelings—and the therapist will remain nonjudgmental.

It is apparent that something good and necessary has been badly twisted. Nothing is wrong with the desire to be accepted as we are, to find someone who despite seeing our ugliness refuses to retreat from us. We all want that. We need it. And the good news of the gospel is that through His death and resurrection, Christ has made it possible for God Himself to see all that we are and yet accept us.

Our longing for a relationship in which we feel secure is legitimate. But when that longing leads us into sharing more and more of who we are in the hope that our Christian brothers and sisters will accept us, we have taken a wrong turn in the road. We come to depend more on each other than on God for the acceptance we need.

When that happens, our fellowship becomes something other than what God intended. The emphasis on sharing in many churches often misses the meaning of *koinonia,* our shared life in Christ. Sharing, as commonly understood, places a premium on emotional honesty *without the framework of commitment to God and to others' welfare.* That is a serious problem.

Consider what might happen if a congregation set about to develop intimate relationships through bold disclosure of their previously disguised emotions. Perhaps the pastor has persuasively exhorted the saints to become warmly unified, preaching as though the text read, "Do not forsake assembling together, but encourage one another by honestly sharing yourselves with each other."

During the fellowship period following the evening service, a woman strides purposefully toward another, takes a deep breath, and shares, "You know, I've never been fully honest with you. You've called me several times a week for months. And I've always said I welcomed your calls and enjoyed them. But that's not true. I have endured your tiresome chatter and catty complaints because I thought I should, but now I see I was just being phony. So I wanted to set the record straight."

In another corner of the fellowship hall, a man thoughtfully sips his coffee, returns the cup to its saucer, and turns to another man standing near. "George, listen. I've got to be honest with you. You asked me to play golf with you next week and I agreed. I've said yes to that invitation a dozen times, but only because I didn't have the guts to be honest. I don't enjoy spending four hours playing golf with you. Your childish temper when you miss a putt, the way you question my score, and your endless run of stupid jokes really get to me. I guess I should have been open about these feelings months ago."

The disease of sharing soon reaches epidemic proportions. All members of the congregation (with the exception of a few self-controlled misfits) are busily ripping off their masks, bravely risking whatever consequences may come as they openly share who they really are. Renaissance man in modern form: bold, fearless, assertive, self-affirming. The problem of surface community has been solved. Now there is deep hostility and division.

The example, I admit, is a bit overdone, but the point is not. The intended remedy of total openness produces difficulties far worse than the problem it was meant to correct. *Total openness replaces surface community with fractured community and eventually no community.* It is not the answer to the problem of layered fellowship.

Christians do live a shared life. We are all partakers of the divine nature, we are indwelt by the same Spirit, we serve the same Lord, we champion the same cause, we obey the same Book, and we anticipate the same destiny. In our fellowship, we are to experience the reality of our common heritage. But we have cheapened the idea of sharing to the point where sharing now means to *exhibit ourselves* rather than to *demonstrate Christ to one another.*

Because the word *sharing* has become a common word in our evangelical vocabulary—heard more often perhaps than words like *holiness, lordship, obedience,* and *discipline,*—I want to highlight the dangers of emphasizing sharing as a means of promoting an encouraging community. At least two warnings must be sounded:

1. *Sharing feelings without a prior and overriding commitment to the welfare of the other leads to disunity, not unity.*

One of the great problems of our day is poor impulse control, or in everyday language, lack of willpower and self-discipline. The lists of top ten best-sellers at any given time usually include several titles about dieting. Why the popularity of books dealing with a practice requiring self-control? Modern men and women seem powerless to resist their internal urges. Salivating at the sight of a cookie leads irresistibly to eating it.

Yet the problem lies not just with food. Sincere Christian men yield to their lusts and furtively sneak a peek at *Playboy* magazine while waiting their turn in the barber's chair. Homemakers struggle with the temptation to put off folding laundry and to view a soap opera instead. The compelling desire to relax before completely finishing a household chore is strong—and the laundry remains unfolded.

We are driven by the strong winds of desire. Yet Paul reminds us that we no longer live in the lusts of the flesh and the desires of the mind; we were dead but have been made alive, quickened by His power and enabled to live obedient lives (Eph. 2:1–10). Why is that for so many more rhetoric than reality?

I am persuaded that one of the key culprits responsible for the lack of self-control is our cultural emphasis on the desirability of self-expression. Our values revolve too much around ideals like openness, authenticity, transparency, assertion, fulfillment, and genuineness. And we tend to regard as outdated concepts like sacrificial giving, self-discipline, self-denying love, obedience, and willing endurance.

As our energy has been directed more toward *expression* than *restraint*, we have suffered a slow, steady erosion of our ability to meaningfully commit ourselves to any direction that runs counter to our urges. For some couples, marriage vows would better reflect their true intent if they were rewritten to read, "I will love you forever, unless perhaps my affection declines."

Any group of people, whether married couples, friends, church staff, or Bible study groups, will run into serious trouble if they emphasize self-disclosure and emotional expression as premium values. A focus on the restraint necessary for surrender to God's purposes strengthens character and enables people to maintain loyalty and commitment through even the stormiest of times.

Without a solid foundation of commitment to restraining oneself in the interests of another's welfare, sharing feelings amounts to nothing more than falsely courageous self-centeredness. Just as physical nudity without marital commitment leads to immorality, so personal nudity without commitment to the other's welfare leads eventually to a fractured relationship. At best an artificial oneness results, which will be only temporary.

   2. *When people give priority to honest sharing, their objective becomes to develop personally comfortable and fulfilling relationships rather than relationships in which others are encouraged to lead a Christ-centered life.*

The paradox of Christianity is that self-fulfillment comes through self-denial. The joys of Christian fellowship are not exhausted when we find someone we like. Relationships have a much deeper basis than mutual enjoyment.

In his first epistle, the apostle John teaches that Christian fellowship does not involve merely lateral relationships between people, but also includes fellowship with the Father and the Son (1 John 1:3). We speak of fellowship with Christ, but too often the profound implications of that concept are lost in our desire to feel comfortable with other people.

We must catch the idea that time spent with one another can somehow enrich our relationship with Christ, in much the same way that two mature children feel closer to their parents after discussing with each other how much their parents mean to them. Relationships with one another can be enjoyable and fulfilling—

and they should be. But the basis of our fellowship is *our shared life in Christ*. Relationships must be regarded as opportunities to promote a fuller appreciation of Christ through mirroring Christ to one another, treating each other as valuable bearers of the image of God, and accepting one another in spite of shortcomings. Too often we view relationships as nothing more than a chance to feel comfortable and to experience a measure of fulfillment.

A young pastor had spent more than a year studying group counseling. Part of his study included participating in a group committed to the value of honest emotional expression. A young woman in the group warmly affirmed the pastor every time he shared. It felt good.

When he came to my office, prodded by a tearful wife, he said, "I just don't feel good about myself when I'm with my wife. When I share who I am with her, she is critical or indifferent. But now I have met someone who gives me a deep sense of fulfillment. I can share all that I am with her and she will accept me. I see no reason to remain in a relationship that is empty when I've tasted the joys of a truly honest and loving relationship. I believe God would have me experience the warmth of love rather than the hypocrisy of my marriage."

Notice this man's moral code. I call it the Morality of Fulfillment: *the rightness of what we do can be measured by the quality of emotions our behavior generates.* Simply stated, If it feels good, do it.

FULFILLMENT THROUGH OBEDIENCE

Biblical morality insists that fulfillment is available through obedience—which is sometimes painful. It is impossible to hold firmly to biblical morality when the value of openness and honest sharing is esteemed more highly than the value of commitment. When people attempt to rid themselves of layers by honestly sharing what they feel, the consequences loom large:

1. A false intimacy at best, but more often friction and increased distance; and
2. A thoroughly self-centered search for fulfillment through relationship (which denies the sufficiency of relationship with Christ) and a disastrous shift from biblical morality.

C. S. Lewis once said that the basic laboratory for knowing God is the Christian community. When that community is a surface one, it fails to serve its purpose. And when we try to deepen community through total openness, our fellowship not only fails to move us toward God, but gets in our way.

SUMMARY

Christians must learn how to encourage one another with their words. Words cannot encourage when people are shielding themselves from hurt by wrapping themselves in protective layers. Words motivated by a need to protect are self-serving and therefore nonencouraging. Only words of love can encourage. Layer-to-layer fellowship must be eliminated for real community, characterized by love and mutual concern, to develop.

The remedy for layer-to-layer fellowship is not to rip off our layers and courageously expose to one another all that we are and feel. Though we must expose ourselves before God and openly confess our sinfulness to Him, total openness with people is a mistake generally motivated by a desire to have others accept us as we are. We are to depend only on God for the acceptance we need.

Total openness as a basic approach to relationships will produce selfish preoccupation with one's own happiness, and division and tension in relationships. We must find another answer for the problem of surface community.

5
Total Commitment: The Right Solution

The foregoing chapters have shown that developing an encouraging community is no simple matter. One-two-three formulas will not work when the objective is to meaningfully and enduringly help people. Congregations have tried many programs to promote better relationships within the church family, but programs are not the answer. Supernaturally enabled love is. But we often miss the route to that love.

Consider the following. A group of God's people gather together with a sincere, determined desire to live out the reality of their faith through Christian community. They long to know Christ with a passion that renders all other desires incidental. After much prayer and study, they conclude that their first priority must be to become a mutually encouraging fellowship. With strong resolve they pledge to make every effort to stimulate one another to love and good deeds.

A practical member of the group interrupts the flow of the meeting by saying, "We are agreed that we must encourage one another. But I'm not exactly certain what I am to do that would be encouraging." The others ponder this and then agree that the point is well taken. How do Christians encourage one another?

Everyone in the group agrees to read, think, and talk to resource people about it in order to find the answer to the question. After a month's research, the group pools its findings. They conclude that most people simply do not listen to one another. If they are to take seriously the value of people as bearers of the divine image, Christians must treat people as people. The group lists eye contact, open-ended questions, quality time together, reflection of feelings, nondefensive debate, clarifying what was heard, and other conversational strategies. These will, they hope, communicate respect and value for one another and thus be encouraging.

For a while, the experiment proceeds surprisingly well. A surge of warmth and closeness fills the group. Fellowship times are rich. Soon, however, the intimacy seems to peak; then unexpected tensions, which verbal techniques seem powerless to check, begin to spread through the body. The members watch their community disintegrate and wonder what went wrong.

Many church bodies have suffered a similar experience. First, a determination to develop a close family atmosphere seems to bear fruit for a time. Then a gradual loss of oneness leaves numbers of Christians puzzled, discouraged, empty, and disillusioned.

THE STARTING POINT

The problem for these people, I believe, is a wrong starting point in putting together an encouraging fellowship. Identifying and mastering conversational techniques is not the place to begin. If a church body really means to get on with the job of encouraging one another, it must first look long and hard at the nature of existing relationships. Careful scrutiny will uncover a core difficulty that merely improving interpersonal skills will not even touch.

Within the heart of people lurks a deep fear that their longing to be treated as valuable may never be met. They cherish a fear of rejection and disrespect and feeling insignificant. A natural concern for personal safety prompts people to clothe themselves with emotional layers—protective coatings to shield themselves from insult and criticism, masks with which to greet each other, facades designed to prevent embarrassment or ridicule, contrived appearances which hide parts they find unacceptable.

These layers are fixed stubbornly in place. Sharpened techniques and surface friendliness offer no more hope of dislodging them than a pea shooter holds for toppling a skyscraper. Listening and affirming skills have no enduring value if spoken from one layer to another. Distance remains. The protection intended to block out *rejecting words* also prevents *encouraging words* from reaching to the core of people. If churches are to become truly encouraging communities, the first order of business is to do something about surface community.

We saw in chapter 4 that stripping away layers and tactlessly expressing all our feelings to one another is not a successful way to deal with surface community. What is the solution?

Note the apostle Paul's words to the Ephesians:

> Let no unwholesome word proceed from your mouth, but only such a word as is good for edification according to the need of the moment, that it may give grace to those who hear (Eph. 4:29).

In this verse Paul introduces us to a solution for our relational problems that is so radical, we stumble over its simplicity. As I understand Paul's words, nothing less is required of us than that every word out of our mouths be consistent with the purpose of building up our listeners. We are permitted to utter nothing that compromises or interferes with that single, comprehensive objective.

Paul's solution to the problem is not to throw off inhibition and expose all that we are. Rather, he instructs us to understand the fears and defenses and needs of other people and *to become committed, not to sharing ourselves, but to sharing the Lord by ministering to those needs.* This is consistent with Paul's admonitions elsewhere to regard others as more important than oneself (as in Phil. 2:3–4).

It sounds deceptively simple: Total Commitment rather than Total Openness. Instead of expressing what I feel in an effort to remove my layers, I am to be concerned with speaking words that reach beneath others' layers and quiet others' fears.

But there is a substantial obstacle to getting on with this solution of Total Commitment. Paul's idea requires that we develop a very definite *motivation,* that we exercise control over the *purpose* of our words. He does not tell us what words to say; he tells us what the motivation behind our words should be.

This is a disturbing twist. We are to be less concerned with *what* we say and more concerned with *why* we say it. But it is so much simpler to merely do the right thing rather than to develop the right motive. Not only is our reservoir of available motivation badly polluted with selfishness and independence, but the real reasons behind our actions are difficult to discern. Our hearts are deceitful and wicked above all else. We are marvelously capable of convincing ourselves that our true purpose is one thing when in fact it is quite another.

Sentences like "Honey, I really love you" may be prompted by the hidden purpose of hearing similar words returned. Or "I really appreciate what you did for me" might well be translated "I want you to do it again." A simple greeting such as "Hi, nice to see you" may actually be an effort to ease one's own social nervousness rather than to convey sincere warmth. Without our being aware, what we say may be designed to achieve something we are after even when the words themselves appear nobly centered on others.

The Bible calls us to ruthless self-examination. But apart from supernatural help our efforts will be futile. We will merely become confused, discouraged, and annoyed. Only God can truly discern the hidden motives of our hearts. The two-edged sword of His Word is the Spirit's instrument for revealing to us our inner thoughts and intents (Heb. 4:12).

We are to be emotionally naked and layer-free with God, fully exposed in all that we are. Hebrews 4:13 says, "There is no creature hidden from His sight, but all things are open and laid bare to the eyes of Him with whom we have to do." The word translated "laid bare" has the idea of our heads being jerked back with our throats vulnerable to whatever injury our assailant might wish to inflict. God knows us as we are. We are to participate in the process of being known, to become consciously vulnerable to a holy God.

Unhurried moments of serious contemplation, guided and controlled by the Spirit speaking through Scripture, are an absolute prerequisite in discerning and straightening out our motivation. We must become sensitively alert to our real goal as we interact with people. Otherwise we cannot be obedient to Paul's command to be governed by the motive to minister.

Layered fellowship has only one solution that creates opportunities for real encouragement: Total commitment to be God's instrument in other people's lives. And nothing less than Spirit-led and Bible-provoked self-examination will enable us to recognize whether our words are self-serving or prompted by the desire to minister.

The solution of total commitment therefore compels us to deal with the problem of our motivation. But it confronts us with a new dilemma.

WHO WILL ENCOURAGE US?

We may develop the ability to discern our hidden motives sensitively and to commit ourselves meaningfully to the goal of ministry. But what are we to do with *our* needs and hurts? How do we handle the fears and longing for acceptance that still prompt us to dress up in layers? The solution of total commitment offers a basis for speaking words designed to encourage others, but who will encourage us? We can drive a car a long distance, but at some point we need to fill the gas tank. We can give and give and give, but unless we get something in return, the car will sputter and stop in the middle of the road. Our emotional gas tanks need filling occasionally.

Like most people, I often feel drained and worn down when I come home from work. Sometimes I am especially burdened by a sense of failure in my counseling—as when a couple whom I have counseled for months have just called it quits. As I cross the threshold of my home, I am really in no mood to minister. I long for a quiet twenty minutes with the sports section of the evening paper and a relaxing dinner with light and pleasant conversation.

My wife greets me, "Hi, honey, how was your day?" I respond with an audible sigh. "I'm beat. What's for dinner?"

Think about the *purpose* of my words. Perhaps I want my wife to recognize my drained condition and treat me with sympathy. The audible sigh is intended to be her cue to hold the news about the broken refrigerator until another time. My needs, not hers, receive priority.

But the apostle Paul tells me that I am wrong and have the situation reversed. My wife's needs, not mine, are to be my first concern. I am to say nothing that compromises my commitment to being used of God in her life.

Suppose that as I enter the home I remind myself of my commitment to my wife. Everything else remains the same: I am tired and discouraged, and my wife greets me, "How are you?" I now respond with "Honey, my day was really difficult, and I'm feeling down. I would really love a few minutes to recover before I join the family."

Nothing in these words is necessarily inconsistent with the purpose of ministry. If I am consciously committed to the goal of meeting my wife's needs, then my words satisfy Paul's criterion. If she at that moment were to make known pressing difficulties facing her, then my commitment would be to respond. And God's grace would make an adequate response possible.

But still, through all my efforts to live consistently with the motive of ministry, I remain acutely aware of my own emotional needs. Suppose a man's wife reacted to his request for a few minutes of recuperative quietness by snapping, "You always think your day is tougher than mine! I'd like to see you try to keep this house clean, answer the blasted phone fifty times, keep the refrigerator stocked at today's prices, and survive an army of noisy kids roaring in and out of the front door all day. When do I get a chance to relax?"

How should a husband respond to that? If we keep our Bibles closed and our consciences quiet, a few choice answers may come to mind. But with our Bibles opened to Ephesians 4, and our consciences open to the Spirit's guidance, what advice can we give to the beleaguered husband? The question reduces to this: *How are we to maintain the goal of ministry to someone else when our own needs are crying for satisfaction?*

For the answer to this hard question, we must distinguish between two concepts: *goal* and *desire*.

GOAL VS. DESIRE

A *goal* may be defined as a purpose to which a person is unalterably committed. He assumes unconditional responsibility for a goal, and it can be achieved if he is willing to work at it.

A *desire* may be defined as something wanted that cannot be obtained without the cooperation of another person. It is an objective for which a person can assume no responsibility, because it is beyond his control. Reaching a desire must never become the motivating purpose behind behavior, because then a person is assuming responsibility for something he cannot fulfill on his own.

A certain friend never seems to grasp the point of my position whenever we get into a discussion. Sometimes I have wondered if he respects my thinking enough to pay real attention to what I say. For some time I have felt a maddening sense of frustration whenever our conversation turns to matters on which we disagree. Why? What is my frustration?

Consider what the purpose of my words might be. Perhaps I am insisting that my friend understand my ideas, not necessarily agree with them. My words then become an effort to reach an objective that I cannot control. I cannot force him to understand;

far less can I make him *want* to understand. Yet, having him understand my ideas became my goal. My motivation is wrong.

Perhaps my friend's refusal to listen represents his layer protecting him from dealing with matters he chooses not to face. Certainly my strenuous efforts to win understanding are my layers designed to shield me from the pain of feeling misunderstood. By the apostle Paul's standards, my words are unwholesome, useless, and worthless—thoroughly nonencouraging. I show no commitment at all to my friend.

My *goal* of inducing him to listen is an objective that violates my definition of a goal, but it comfortably fits the idea of a *desire*. Of course I *want* him to listen to me. That is not sinful in itself. But to *demand* that he listen, to somehow assume that I *need* him to listen, is sinful.

I have to reconnect a few mental wires to make it my goal to understand him as well as I can and to state my position as clearly as I can. This dual purpose—to understand him and to speak clearly—can be achieved with or without his cooperation. My desire that he hear me has to be kept in place as just that—a desire, not a goal.

Goals are objectives toward which we should work. Desires are objectives for which we should pray. I have to labor to understand my friend and to present my thinking nondefensively. And as I work toward that goal, I pray that one day he might understand me. *Pray for desires. Work for goals.*

Whether we are tired husbands greeted by harried wives, or unappreciated wives neglected by workaholic husbands, or lonely singles who cannot find a niche, or friendly Christians who are regularly snubbed—whoever we are, we must carefully sort out our goals and desires. We can legitimately long for much-longed-for encouragement—a *desire*—but we must set our wills to pursue the purpose of encouraging others—a *goal*. We must pray that our desires for encouragement will be satisfied (and trust God for whatever happens), and we must work hard to encourage others. My desire is that *I* be encouraged. My goal is that I do all I can to encourage *others*.

The solution to surface community is total commitment to the *goal* of ministry. But that doesn't solve the whole problem. Suppose my *desires* remain badly unmet. Can I continue to pursue the goal of ministry indefinitely when no one ministers to me? The next chapter deals with that question.

SUMMARY

Total openness will not solve the problem of surface community, but total commitment will.

Total commitment requires that we commit ourselves, not to reducing our fears, but to doing whatever we can to reduce the fears of others, or to fulfill their needs.

The idea of total commitment gets at the motivation behind our words. We are to be more concerned that our purpose is to minister to others than with the specific words we say. Awareness of our motivation requires spiritual insight available only through the study and meditation of Scripture.

We are to commit ourselves to the goal of encouraging others while we acknowledge our desire to be encouraged by others. When our desire to be encouraged is not met, it is difficult to maintain our goal to minister to others—but it is possible.

6
The Character
of an Encourager

W hen we interact as Christians—at lunch, in a Sunday school class, as dinner guests, or over the telephone—we are consciously and consistently to do what does *not* come naturally. We must remind ourselves that our purpose is to minister, and we must commit ourselves afresh to that purpose.

To honor that commitment, however, does not mean that every paragraph we utter has to include a Scripture verse; nor does it mean that we are to adopt a contrived spiritual tone as some people do when they pray. The responsibility to minister does not rob life of its normalcy.

It is good to enjoy a competitive tennis match, to engage in impassioned debate, or to gather with friends in front of a roaring fire to drink hot chocolate. I am not recommending a stiffly pious, brow-creased, contemplative demeanor that scrupulously avoids laughter and casual banter. Nor am I suggesting that every conversation be elevated to a supposed higher plane by liberally sprinkling in phrases like "What a blessing!" or "Praise the Lord!" If these expressions come naturally, that's fine; if not, it's better to leave them out. Forced spirituality is not really spiritual at all.

Christians committed to ministry are to go on preparing meals, chatting with friends, paying bills, and going to work. But amid the routine of life we must maintain a conscious commitment to promote other people's welfare. It is our responsibility as Christians to tune in to the possible impact of our words in every situation and to select only those that reflect a sensitivity to the needs of others. We are to develop, maintain, and nourish the motivation of ministry in all that we do and say.

The apostle Paul underscores the importance of maintaining pure motives when he speaks of the judgment seat of Christ before which all Christians will appear. At the judgment our Lord will uncover the motivation behind everything we have done here on earth, and He will reward us only for the deeds prompted by godly purposes (1 Cor. 4:5). All else will be burned as worthless.

What we do, therefore, is in one sense less important than why we do it. If in greeting a stranger my *goal* is to impress him with my pastoral heart, then my kindness will go unrewarded. It is a fruit of the flesh. If I *desire* that others appreciate my concern for people, but maintain the *goal* of warming the stranger's heart—and if I pursue that goal whether or not my desires are met—then my kindness is a true act of love.

This is a lofty standard. When I contemplate the meaning of proper motivation and God's requirements for me, I throw up my hands in defeat and admit I simply cannot measure up. I find within me a stubborn attitude which demands that others minister to me. It is hard to change that demand into a mere desire. Distinctions between goals and desires are easily stated, but not easily practiced. Yet I am to develop a single-minded determination to pursue the goals that God sets before me. I am somehow to develop the strength of character that enables me to remain committed to ministry, even when it appears that no one is properly ministering to me. Where does this strength of character come from?

I once talked with a man who had spent nearly three years in a concentration camp for prisoners of war. During his confinement he resolved to learn the meaning of our Lord's strange command to "love your enemies and do good to them who despitefully use you." His time in prison provided him with a unique opportunity to test whether the Spirit could forge character of that quality in the hot fires of persecution. And He did. My friend reported that he learned to care genuinely for the welfare of his persecutors.

How can we develop character like that? Most of us cannot manage to love a Christian brother who talks too much, let alone an enemy captor who beats us mercilessly. Yet, if we are to become real encouragers in the body of Christ, we must be strong enough to remain committed to minister to others even when our desires go badly unmet. But how?

THE PROBLEM WITH MINISTRY

When I was a youngster in Pennsylvania, I would love to get up early on cold winter mornings. Before dressing, I would carefully arrange a pillow about five feet away from the heat register that was located on the wall near the floor. I would stretch out with my feet poised in front of the register. With the warm air caressing my naked feet, I felt content and happy, without a worry in the world. *I* enjoyed the heat, and *Dad* paid for it. There was something deeply satisfying about letting another person assume full responsibility for my well-being.

Circumstances are a bit different today. Before our move back to northern climates, my family lived in South Florida for ten years. Whenever our air-conditioning unit switched on, my mind uncontrollably formed images of the electric meter whirling round and round at dizzying, costly speed. It was now my children's turn to be carefree and comfortable while their father sweated over the coolness. Memories of warm air blowing from the heat register during a northern winter remind me how good it feels to utterly abandon ourselves to someone else's care, to depend on another person to provide for us.

The desire to be cared for by someone stronger than oneself is a necessary part of the human condition. Because this longing to abandon ourselves to another person is so strong, we feel a natural resistance to becoming *dependable*. We would rather be *dependent*.

Yet, becoming dependable is precisely what a commitment to ministry requires. In order to minister, I must resist my natural longing to influence others to minister to me.

When we sit still long enough to become aware of ourselves, we can all find an almost sentimental longing to relax in someone else's strength, to feel secure in warmth provided by a loving benefactor. Part of the problem with ministry is this: the more determined I am to minister, the more painfully aware I become of my desire to have someone look after me.

But Paul's command to always concern ourselves with others' needs seems to callously ignore the reality of this heartfelt desire. If I am to be committed to *helping* another, then I am never free to *abandon* myself to another. Yet that is what my soul cries out for. As a child, I never worried about paying the heat bill. That abandonment to parental resources felt good. But to abandon myself to someone requires that I give no thought at all to that person's welfare.

Here is the real problem with this requirement to minister: *I am never permitted to disregard the effect my words have on others.* There is therefore no one on earth—literally no one—to whom I can rightfully abandon myself. I am to see to it that my words are always suited to everyone else's needs. But I don't want to worry about my impact on others; I'd prefer that others concern themselves with their impact on me.

People who take seriously the goal of ministry, and who are careful to prevent their *desires* for receiving ministry from becoming their *goals*, will inevitably encounter a profound loneliness. An awareness develops that although we may share with others, we can never fully depend on others. The Christian committed to ministry will not permit himself to do the very thing that his deepest longings urge him to do. He will not abandon himself to anyone. To do so would violate his commitment to minister.

Even if he were to scrap the purpose of ministry and actively seek to end his loneliness through others' ministry to him, he would find no real satisfaction. The best of friends will inevitably fail us, because of either self-preoccupation or imperfect understanding of our needs. There is no escape. The human condition in its fallen state is a lonely one, and a commitment to minister compounds the problem.

THE SURPRISING VIRTUE OF LONELINESS

But as in the old movies in which the victim has been tied to the railroad tracks by a handlebar-mustached villain, the story isn't over. . . . The God of Remarkable Surprises has once again turned a desperate situation into an opportunity for unparalleled joy. There is a godly solution to the problem of loneliness created by the commitment to minister.

If our words of encouragement are to have substantial impact if our efforts to strengthen each other in the Christian walk are to be more than a pep talk, then we *must* become men and women who not only *know about* God, but actually *know* Him.

I shared a platform once with a certain man who was approaching seventy years of age. l was in my late twenties. My preaching was practical, relevant, and interesting. But his was powerful. The difference was that he knew God in a way that made my relationship with the Deity seem like little more than a hat-tipping acquaintance.

Godly character requires knowing God firsthand. *The route to knowing God eventually passes directly through the valley of profound loneliness.* It is in the times when there is no one but God that we learn to know Him most fully. Those times—those moments of utter aloneness—come only from emptying our lives into the lives of others.

When we *depend* on no one to minister to us, when we thankfully accept the little encouragement coming our way from others, then the soul will feel its deepest longing—to abandon itself to someone perfectly reliable and strong. We will feel profound loneliness. If in that moment we steadfastly refuse to compromise our commitment to minister, if we dependently abandon ourselves to no one, then the loneliness will intensify.

At those moments when the loneliness is greatest, we must turn in desperate dependency to God. We must entrust ourselves so completely to Him that our psychological doom is assured if He fails to respond. Then we will come to know more of Him. Then godly character will grow. His glory bursts through most brightly when the night is darkest. His strength is proven most sufficient when we are weakest. His love penetrates most deeply when we feel unloved.

Sometime ago I was sharing these thoughts with a group of people in another country. After one of my messages, a man in his late twenties approached me with a story he felt impressed to relate. During the previous year, his wife had undergone a double mastectomy because of cancer. From diagnosis through surgery and on to the present, he had struggled to remain strong for his wife, wanting to be a source of encouragement for her. His own pain, confusion, and fear were nearly crippling him emotionally, but he devoted himself to the one purpose of ministering to his wife.

The young man asked me to read Psalm 142 aloud. As I thumbed through my Bible, he told me of the many nights when sleep would not come, nights when—sometimes with his wife, sometimes alone, but always with tears—he would read the words of that psalm in prayer. I found the passage and read these words:

> When my spirit was overwhelmed within me,
> Thou didst know my path (v. 3).
>
> No one cares for my soul.

I cried out to Thee, O Lord;
I said, "Thou art my refuge,
My portion in the land of the living" (vv. 4, 5).

"Give heed to my cry,
For I am brought very low" (v. 6).

"Bring my soul out of prison; . . .
Thou wilt deal bountifully with me" (v. 7).

My voice was unsteady as I read, and my eyes could barely contain the wetness. I realized that I was reading words of life to this young man, words that had been his pathway to deep communion with God.

My mind moved to similar words in Psalm 73:

Whom have I in heaven but thee?
And besides Thee, I desire nothing on earth. . . .
As for me, the nearness of God is my good (vv. 25, 28).

The character of an encourager must be strong. It must be molded and hardened in the fires of loneliness when no one but God is there. And loneliness—that surprising opportunity to know God—comes as we so thoroughly commit ourselves to ministering to others that we depend on God alone to minister to us. His ministry draws us into His very presence so that we can speak to others from holy ground. Then our words have power for good.

SUMMARY

We are to maintain our commitment to minister to others even when others are severely failing in their ministry to us.

The commitment to minister requires that we never fully abandon ourselves to another human being, nor ever wholly depend on someone else to minister to us. Practicing that commitment brings us into touch with our profound need to do what our commitment will not let us do: depend fully on another. The result is the pain of loneliness.

If, during our moments of deepest loneliness, we abandon ourselves completely to God, depending on Him to minister to us, we will meet God. Our deepest parts will be strengthened; our character will become rooted in His resources.

We will then be enabled to continue with our commitment to minister, motivated by our time spent in His presence. Our words will be words of giving, overflowing with the love He has made known to us. Our words will have the power to encourage.

7
When Do We Tell Somebody Else How We Feel?

People who want to become encouragers face a difficult problem when they commit themselves to the goal of ministry in all their interpersonal contacts. The commitment to giving quickly exhausts personal resources and accentuates their own yearnings to receive what they are committed to give.

The resulting loneliness must not drive the encourager to cynicism, withdrawal, diversion, or superficiality. Rather, it must drive him to a despair in which he is utterly shut up to the resources of God. In that loneliness, the *fact* of relationship with Christ becomes a passionately *felt* reality.

Yet, even as he senses God's revitalizing strength, there is still a problem that demands proper handling: would-be encouragers continue to feel troublesome emotions. I suppose there is a depth of fellowship with Christ that drowns all but healthy, constructive emotions; but that sort of spiritual maturity is at best a distant hope for many of us. We may sincerely commit ourselves to the ministry of encouraging others and determine to trust the Lord fully for His ministry to us; but still we are plagued by feelings such as irritation, jealousy, worry, bitterness, and lust.

What is a determined encourager to do when he is really irked by the one he intends to encourage? How do we encourage someone who irritates us? Certainly the ministry of encouragement should extend beyond the circle of people we enjoy. What are we to do when a friend unburdens himself about a lesser disappointment at the same time a personal frustration over shattered hopes is eating away at us? We will not be prone to encourage that person.

Committed ministers of encouragement will experience a variety of emotions that interfere with efforts to encourage. How do we maintain our commitment to encourage others when we ourselves feel negative emotions?

Human beings are capable of handling their emotions in three ways. We will examine these strategies and determine which of them will further the ministry of encouragement. The three strategies are—

1. Repression
2. Expression
3. Acknowledgment and Purposeful Expression

STRATEGY 1: REPRESSION

A godly woman was told by her husband that he was having an affair. He chose to drop the news to his wife as she was preparing to leave for a women's Bible conference in which she was a principal speaker. Although she had been dimly aware that something was amiss in the marriage, the idea of infidelity had never crossed her mind.

She endured the first day of the conference and then called me at midnight. Her manner during the conversation impressed me as peculiar. She told me her story almost as if she were talking about another woman's grief. When I asked her how she felt, she replied, "I just feel so bad for him. He must be going through an awful time."

I winced and asked, "Aren't you angry or hurt? At least a little upset? How come you're tuning in to his struggle when your heart must be breaking?" Her reply—"I just want to be all that I can be for him"—suggested that the apparent givingness of her attitude concealed negative emotions that she preferred not to admit. Several sessions of face-to-face counseling justified my suspicions. Her insides were raging with anger that she was hiding from herself. It required intensive probing with sharp questions to uncover the buried feelings. She had repressed her emotions.

Consider a second example of this strategy for handling emotion. One of my counseling clients had been raised in an ultrafashionable home in which all the children dressed "preppy," had proper dining etiquette, and involved themselves in school politics, usually as leaders.

My patient, a man of twenty-nine, had adjusted well to the

family's standards. He graduated cum laude from law school, his wife was a debutante whose family name graced every social register, and the law firm in which he secured a position gave him an income sufficient to cover payments on a large home and a prestigious car.

The call for an appointment was triggered when he attacked his wife for what he himself described as a trivial complaint about his long working hours. After he attacked her, he backed off and then banged his head against the edge of a bedroom door until his head became a bloody mess. He collapsed in a heap on the floor, sobbing convulsively for nearly twenty minutes. Having no idea what had caused his outburst, he called me for help the next morning.

In both of the cases I have related, my counselees had mastered the art of emotional repression: "I don't want to feel something, so I don't." The woman denied her anger in the name of Christianity, and the young man repressed his for the sake of appearances. Both suffered the consequences of mishandling strong emotions by denying their existence.

Just before the apostle Paul instructs us to watch how we speak, he tells us to "speak truth" to each other and to deal with anger quickly in a way that promotes reconciliation (Eph. 4:25–26). A person feeling anger is on the edge of the precipice of sin. When we are angry, it is easy to sin by dumping our emotions on others without concern for their impact. But to avoid the sin of unchecked expression by *pretending to ourselves* that we are not angry is no solution.

Christians are not to pretend about anything. Whether we lust, worry, covet, resent, or hate, we are to acknowledge the reality of who we are at any given moment. Fully admitting to ourselves and to God that we are angry, or whatever, and permitting our bodies to feel the physical concomitants of strong emotion, is not sin. To do otherwise is foolish.

God calls us to encourage people who sometimes annoy and frustrate us. We will feel angry and upset at times. God calls us to live as imperfect people who must contend with a world filled with problems and disappointments. We will feel tense, discouraged, worried, guilty, and inadequate. In our efforts to become encouragers centered on others, we are not to cap the volcano of smoldering emotions with a lid of pretense and denial. Repressing feelings may create the impression that we are spiritually mature (and we may fool both ourselves and others), but it will not promote genuine maturity. Repression creates pressure and phoniness. People whose strength depends on denying bad feelings cannot speak words that have the power to encourage deeply.

STRATEGY 2: EXPRESSION

Psychologists occasionally talk about something they call "ecclesiogenic neurosis," an emotional disorder that can be traced to an origin in the church. They believe (with some justification) that evangelical churches generally, and fundamentalist churches especially, favor repression as the most acceptable strategy for handling negative emotions. The troubles that follow in the wake of repression are given the label "neuroses."

Assessing the psychological wreckage caused by religious restraint, psychologists are fond of recommending emotional expression as the antidote to emotional repression. If *unexpressed emotions* cause problems, these advocates of self-indulgent catharsis contend, then *expressed emotions* relieve problems. But endorsing the unrestrained ventilation of emotions simply exchanges one disease for a worse one.

Early in my counseling practice I succeeded, after much effort, to help a particularly repressed woman admit to feeling hostile when her husband staggered home drunk in the wee hours of the morning. She arrived for the next session wearing a look of smug satisfaction. "I think I'm cured!" she announced. "When my husband came home two nights ago at two-thirty smelling like a bar, I really got in touch with my anger. I was really steaming! So I waited till he crawled into bed, then I got up, went to my closet, and threw every shoe I own at him. He was too drunk to even move, so I got him good! And I felt a whole lot better."

My client had certainly been cured of repression and had laid hold of its opposite with aplomb. I would hope, however, that no responsible counselor—secular or Christian—would sanction such behavior as progress toward mental health. Releasing emotions without restraint is no improvement over pretending that bad emotions don't exist.

The biblical strategy for handling emotions is neither un-checked expression nor neurotic repression. *Repression* creates psychological tensions that strengthen defensive layers and there-fore interfere with encouragement. *Indiscriminate expression* robs people of the opportunity to experience Christ's strength even when strong emotions rage within. Neither strategy will promote our efforts to become encouragers.

What then are we to do with negative, unloving emotions? How are we to honor our commitment to encourage when problem emotions have somehow crept into our hearts? If it is wrong both to repress and to express, what's left?

STRATEGY 3: ACKNOWLEDGMENT AND PURPOSEFUL EXPRESSION

There are times when it is right to express strong, ungentle emotions. An obvious biblical example is our Lord's driving the moneychangers out of the temple (Mark 11:12ff.; John 2:12ff.). There are others. The apostle Paul wrote stinging words of rebuke to the Corinthian church. And when Peter fell prey to the influence of Judaizers, Paul "opposed him to his face" (Gal. 2:11), an expression hardly suggesting a soft, gracious exchange of words. In the Old Testament, the imprecatory psalms are full of scathing words about enemy people—note especially Psalm 137:9.

Not just anger but profound grief and agony can also be rightly made known to others. The friends of Lazarus witnessed Christ's tears as He stood by the tomb. Later, Peter, James, and John might have heard words full of deep pain fall from the Savior's lips as they stayed awake with Him at Gethsemane. To the Thessalonians and others, Paul freely expressed the emotional distress he felt as he worried over the church's spiritual state.

It is clear from these examples that negative emotions can and should be shared in a biblical way. But when? How? We must first acknowledge to ourselves and to God whatever we feel (thus avoiding the error of repression), and we must then discern when it is morally permissible to express our feelings (avoiding the error of unchecked expression). The question becomes, When is it right to tell somebody else how we feel?

An illustrative suggestion for handling strong emotions is recorded in Ezekiel 24:15–18. In this passage God informs Ezekiel that He is about to take the prophet's beloved wife. After announcing His intentions, God immediately instructs Ezekiel to refrain from any outward display of grief. He tells Ezekiel to "groan silently."

In commanding Ezekiel to *groan* silently, God was not recommending repression. The prophet was not to pretend that his wife's death generated no sorrow. In groaning *silently*, however, he was to withhold external expression of that sorrow. Why? Is it wrong to mourn publicly at a spouse's funeral? Why was it wrong for Ezekiel to weep at his wife's graveside when it was acceptable for Christ to weep at the tomb of Lazarus?

When the Lord wept, His tears in no way interfered with the Father's purpose in the event. In fact, the tears furthered it. But for Ezekiel to cry would have obscured the message that God wanted to declare to His rebellious people, namely, that the coming judgment for their sin was so terrible that by comparison not even the death of a beloved wife merited a tear.

The principle that emerges is this: we are to acknowledge fully before God what we feel and to experience internally the full weight of our emotions; but *we may express our acknowledged emotions only when such expression will further God's purposes.* To state this principle more simply, we are to handle our emotions by (1) privately acknowledging our feelings to God and to ourselves, and (2) subordinating the expression of our feelings, in both timing and manner, to the goal of ministry.

Because some believe that denying release to strong emotions can be psychologically harmful, it is important to understand a critical point: emotions cause problems, not when they remain *unexpressed,* but when they remain *unacknowledged.* The cure for repression does not require total expression of every emotion. The opposite of repression is not expression. Rather, it is acknowledgment: a conscious, subjective experiencing of whatever emotion exists.

Psychological problems can develop in another manner, however. Suppose someone admits that he feels a certain way, but he refuses to express emotion out of fear (and not out of concern for God's purposes). Expressing our feelings can make us vulnerable to personally threatening consequences. Consider how this might happen.

A church member confided in me that he was furious with the leader of his weekly Bible study group. There was no problem with repression; he knew what he felt. When I inquired as to what he was doing with his anger, he replied, "Nothing. We're friends with him and his wife. Our wives are especially close. If I told him how I felt and if that messed up my wife's friendship with them, I'd never hear the end of it from her. It isn't worth the potential hassle."

This man was neither repressing nor expressing his anger. He knew what he felt, but he was not making it known. Yet his reason for not expressing his anger had nothing to do with a commitment to God's purposes. Instead, he was fearful of the unpleasant consequences he might suffer.

Notice this man's confusion between goal and desire. His *goal* should be to please God and edify the offending brother, but in fact his true goal was to avoid hassles. Hassle-avoidance perhaps qualifies as a *desire,* but it is not a worthy goal.

What would an effective encourager do if he were the angry man? He must not repress his anger; nor should he express it with no thought of ministry; nor should he choose not to express his anger out of fear of consequences. The principle of Acknowledgment and Purposeful Expression might be worked out in four steps in this situation:

First, he should spend time with the Lord, rearranging his goals and desires and reaffirming his commitment to the goal of ministry;

Second, he must affirm that ministry is his goal by searching for ways to express kindness to the group leader;

Third, after discussing the matter with his wife—to assure her of his sensitivity to the delicate issues involved and to invite her counsel on his timing and wording—he should share his feelings with the offending brother with the stated purpose of bringing reconciliation;

Fourth, whether his brother becomes indignant and withdraws, or is apologetic and warm, he must actively forgive his brother by continuing to pray for him and looking for appropriate ways of demonstrating love and concern.

What should encouragers do with their feelings? A person should never repress, but always fully acknowledge his feelings to God and to himself. This allows him to privately experience the full weight of the emotion (as Nehemiah 1:4 demonstrates). Then, with a reaffirmed and conscious commitment to the goal of ministry, he should decide whether the expression of those feelings will further God's purposes; counsel from an unbiased, mature Christian is often helpful in making that difficult decision. If expression is judged to be appropriate, he should make the feelings known to the relevant person; if not, he should choose to deny them expression as an act of service to God.

SUMMARY

Most of us, no matter how mature we may be spiritually, will experience negative emotions like anger, worry, or greed.

Encouragers must realize that emotions can be (1) repressed, (2) expressed, or (3) acknowledged and selectively expressed according to the goal of ministry.

Repression involves pretending, and the Bible never sanctions denying reality. Expression with no thought of another's welfare is selfish indulgence. Both repression and indiscriminate expression are unbiblical strategies for handling negative emotions.

Encouragers must allow themselves to feel the full weight of their emotions, but then subordinate their expression to the purposes of God.

Refusing to express emotions for any reason other than voluntary submission to the goal of ministry will create personal difficulties. Chosen expression of acknowledged emotions within the framework of ministry is the biblical strategy for handling negative emotions.

Our concern in the rest of the book will be with the process of encouragement itself.

Part II
THE PROCESS OF ENCOURAGEMENT

8
How Encouragement Works

It is a mistake to think of encouragement as a set of specific words or phrases. Encouragement depends less on which words we use than on the motivation behind them. Words that encourage are (1) inspired by love, and (2) directed toward fear. These two conditions must be met for words to encourage. Let us look at these conditions in more detail.

> Condition 1: Words that encourage are prompted by love, not by fear; that is, the words spoken must never function as a layer for the speaker;
>
> Condition 2: Words that encourage are aimed not at another's layers with the intent of rearranging them, but rather at another's hidden fear with the intent of reducing it.

Words spoken from a layer to a layer do not encourage (Figure 1). Words spoken from your layer to another's fear (Figure 2) may have some temporary encouragement value—for example, when a person whose layer is "pastoral warmth" speaks with insight and love to a troubled friend. Similarly, words spoken from a heart of love to another's layer (Figure 3) may do some good. When a truly loving person unwisely offers superficial advice to someone who is hurting, some level of encouragement may occur.

Real encouragement, however, occurs when words are spoken from a heart of love to another's recognized fear (Figure 4).

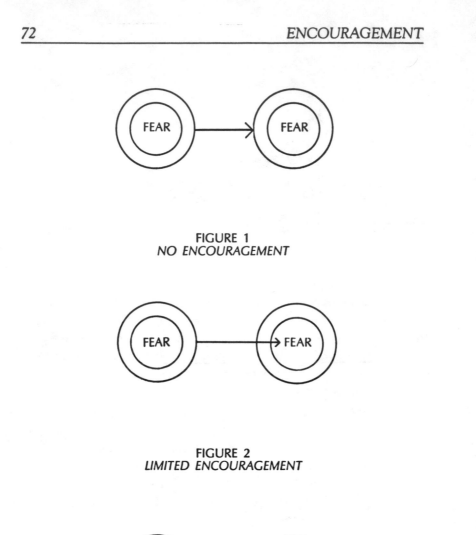

FIGURE 1
NO ENCOURAGEMENT

FIGURE 2
LIMITED ENCOURAGEMENT

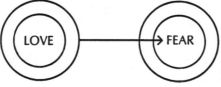

FIGURE 3
LIMITED ENCOURAGEMENT

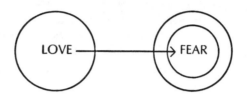

FIGURE 4
TRUE ENCOURAGEMENT

CONDITION 1: PROMPTED BY LOVE

Countless sermons have used for illustration the various news accounts of good citizens who witnessed a brutal assault on an innocent passerby and did nothing to help. The usual punch line of the anecdote, well-worn but still penetrating, is the reason offered by the onlookers for their lack of response: "We didn't want to get involved—too risky."

Christianity *is* involvement, from beginning to end. There is no greater example of loving involvement than the Incarnation, in which God literally became human for the express purpose of enduring the terrible punishment that divine justice requires of sinful people.

The ascended Savior, still incarnate and therefore able to relate to us in all our testings and trials, calls us to a life of involvement in other people's lives. We are told to rejoice with rejoicers, weep with weepers, restore the unspiritual, admonish the unruly, strengthen the weak—in sum, by words and deeds encourage others to press on in their pursuit of holiness (Rom. 12). The only motivation that will stir us to reach into others' lives with encouragement is love. Our words must come from unfeigned, genuine love for God and people.

But we hold back. Like the frightened observer of a crime, we seek to remain uninvolved. We maintain a comfortable distance by withdrawing behind our layers. We may react to people with criticism, analysis, gossip, interest, perhaps even concern, but we rarely demonstrate the kind of involvement modeled for us in the

Incarnation. Everything but involvement comes naturally. Our instinctive response to an annoying brother is irritation. People who don't agree with our thinking seem narrow-minded. Irresponsibility in co-workers or roommates provokes criticism. It simply is not natural to react to another's layers with loving concern.

Why are uninvolvement and distance our natural responses? Why is involved interest foreign to us? Why do we tend to relate to people from behind our layers? Even though we sense a longing for intimate relationships (if we take the time to look at ourselves), we still find ways to keep our distance. When someone offends us and our angry feelings create a wall, we may explode at the offender or sulk or avoid dealing with the problem. Many people have developed real skill in steering conversations away from sensitive areas into the safe territory of trivia. Why do we have this stubborn tendency to relate to people from behind defensive layers? Until we diagnose and remedy this problem, we will not develop a ministry of encouragement.

One of my best friends caused me deep concern some time ago. From observing him during times of fellowship with others, I knew he was handling an important matter in his life rather badly. The problem was snowballing: the more he mishandled the situation, the worse it became, and the more ineffectively he dealt with it. It required little discernment to realize that he was very discouraged. His difficulties seemed unconquerable. I wanted to encourage him, to stimulate him to love and good works. But I felt an urge to back away, to pray for him without speaking to him about the matter. Why?

A little reflection showed me clearly that I was not eager to risk upsetting a rather comfortable and pleasant relationship. I preferred the familiar ease of our casual conversation to the uncertain repercussions of an attempt to discuss a ticklish topic. For a time I consoled myself with the rationalization that words like "How ya' doing?" and "It's good to see you" were at least mildly encouraging. Finally I admitted to myself that descriptions of food offered no help to a hungry friend; instead, they would be cruel, especially if my refrigerator were well stocked.

Convicted of my selfish fears, I prayed for an opportunity to speak directly to my friend about the matter. I looked for ways to address the subject. One day, when his gloomy expression matched his discouraged words, I seized the opportunity and told him of my concern. I spoke clearly and to the point, exposing for both of us precisely what I thought was happening inside him. Because the Spirit of God filled the interchange with a love that precluded criticism, the effect was encouragement for both of us—for me because of his openness to change, for him because of the evidence of my care and concern. I wondered afterward why it was so hard. I concluded again that the obstacle was fear that I might lose something I valued and enjoyed. I feared that my involvement might precipitate uncomfortable tensions. It was a fear that, like all fears but the fear of God, is preoccupied with self.

A counseling client of mine was known to all her acquaintances as a friendly, gracious, and delightful person. If anyone seemed like a sure candidate to become an effective encourager, it was she. But she had a problem: no one felt especially close to her. Everyone enjoyed her presence, but none would claim her as a "best friend." Her ready smile and eager hospitality appeared to invite relationship, but their effect was to block it. She came to see me because of loneliness and an empty feeling that had deteriorated into depression.

She acknowledged in the safe environment of my soundproof office that she was bitter toward her mother, jealous of her husband's use of time, worried sick about her children, and put out with thoughtless friends who regularly impose on her kindness. Then she said timidly, "If I told anyone how I really felt, I'm afraid nobody would like me."

Contrary to first impressions, this woman's sweetness and charm were not the expression of love. Actually they were nothing more than manipulative layers designed to protect herself from hurt. Thoughtful words from her mouth had no real power to encourage. They came from a layer, not from a heart of love. She was not involved at all with people in giving, vulnerable relationships. She lived in an isolated castle, sealed off from the world by an uncrossable moat of fear-motivated graciousness that set people at a distance.

We must remember that words motivated by fear have no power to encourage. They may cover a wound, but they never heal it. Only love promotes healing. Words spoken from a layer are worthless—the unprofitable words mentioned in Ephesians 4:29. If words are to qualify as encouraging, they must spring freely from love. But how do we shift from fear to love, from speaking words out of layers to speaking words out of love?

I spoke with a man who rarely expressed anger to anyone,

especially to his wife. He had long regarded his gentle manner as a well-developed virtue until he came to realize that his unwillingness to express anger reflected, not love, but a fear of losing a relationship. This is the nub of the matter. It is most natural to maintain a commitment to our own interpersonal comfort, a commitment that creates a feeling of uneasiness whenever we are tempted to risk authentic involvement in someone else's life. Most of us are simply afraid to threaten our sense of comfortable well-being.

I recently sat next to a young woman in Sunday school class whom I did not know. Just before the class began, I introduced myself and asked her name. During the lesson she offered an embarassingly wrong answer to a rather elementary question. The teacher stumbled a bit in his efforts to overcome the awkwardness of the moment, saying something like, "Well, yes, that would be a good answer if the question were different." I saw the woman blush, smile sheepishly, adjust her skirt, and die a thousand deaths. Here was an obvious need for a few encouraging words.

As the classtime drew to a close, I felt a nagging resistance to my plan to encourage her. "Say hi to your friends," I told myself. "She'll be O.K.; she doesn't look embarrassed now anyway. She's probably forgotten all about her wrong answer, or at least I'll bet she wants to. I'd probably make matters worse by talking to her. Nobody likes sympathy. And I really should talk to the teacher about that one point he made that struck me."

Now, what would deter someone like me—who makes his living by talking to hurting people—from speaking a few simple, encouraging words to a young woman so clearly in need of them? The reason is fear. Hardly a terrifying fright of rejection, but a mild fear of spending a few moments in what could be an uncomfortable situation. It was safer to chat about biblical exegesis with the teacher.

Whether the cause of fear is major rejection or mild discomfort, the final solution is the same: *I must be willing to hurt (greatly or minimally), to suffer loss (be it everything or a few moments of social ease).* Only when I accept what I fear, resolving that I am willing to endure whatever may happen, will the fear lose its power (1 John 4:18). The perfect love of Christ provides me with what I need to face my fears. In Christ I have a relationship I cannot lose, a relationship sufficient to sustain me if all others fail. I have an unbreakable safety net beneath me as I venture across the tightrope of involving myself in other people's lives.

When I declare myself, by an act of will, to be willing to lose all human relationship (approval, recognition, love, etc.) if obedience to God requires it, I will be freed from the entanglements of fear. And only when I am freed from the fear of losing a relationship will my motivation approach the reality of love. When I encounter an embarrassed stranger in Sunday school or a close friend who is seriously mishandling his problems, my words will have the power to encourage if they are prompted by love. Notice the paradox: *To love a person, I must be willing to lose my relationship with him.* Dependently holding onto anyone or anything but God is, in its final form, idolatry. Idolatry is at root a fear of the wrong god.

The practical outworking of these lofty thoughts is not a complicated matter. As I contemplate speaking to the blushing woman in Sunday school, I must take my thoughts firmly in hand and control them. I must think, "Yes, if I approach her, there might be a moment of social awkwardness. She might even react badly and walk away. I certainly would be more comfortable if I chose to avoid her, but comfort is not my goal. God's will is. I really do want to be His instrument of blessing. And if I do try to encourage her, not only will I be obedient to God and likely a help to her, but my relationship with God will deepen. That's worth whatever the cost. Hang it all, fear or no fear, I will see what I can do to encourage her. She looks as though she could use it." Words that have the power to encourage deeply are words motivated by love, not by fear.

CONDITION 2: DIRECTED TOWARD FEAR

To be encouraging, words must be prompted by love. That's the first condition. The second condition is equally important: they must be directed to fear. From my love to another's fear— that's the formula. Words of rebuke, exhortation, suggestion, instruction, or sympathy must all meet these two conditions if they are to further God's purposes and qualify as words of encouragement.

Targeting our words toward the fear of another is an easily stated but often misunderstood concept. Too many people reason like this: "All this encouragement business about warmth and supportiveness and acceptance is really off the mark. It fails to

address the real problem and evidences a weak view of sin. People
need less affirmation and more exhortation to put off the old man
and put on the new."

People with "executive personalities" (who rarely have close
friends) mercilessly pound others about their responsibilities. They
apply pressure in every available way to compel others to have
devotions, witness, attend church, and tithe. Some people,
depending on their temperament, conform to the pressure and
appear to move along nicely on the road to spiritual maturity.
Others rebel. In either case, little heart movement toward God
takes place.

The still-popular cult of Christian self-love, whose cardinal
teaching is "You must learn to love yourself," leads the reaction to
the harsh exhorters by swinging to the other extreme. "We just
need to be warm and unconditionally caring. Exhortation, calls to
discipline, and pressure to make commitments are all counterpro-
ductive to spiritual growth. People need an atmosphere of loving
acceptance for growth to occur. Only in the context of love will
personal maturity develop."

These people come dangerously close to buying into human-
ism, an unbiblical philosophy that affirms the inherent goodness of
man and argues that problems result when society thwarts the
expression of that goodness by an oppressive system of laws and
sanctions. Christians need to divorce themselves from this idea by
recognizing the radical results of mankind's fall into sin. The truth
is, people have no natural tendency to conform their lives to the
character of God. Straying from the path of righteousness is as
natural to us as bucking is to a bronco.

Spiritual regeneration by the Holy Spirit provides us with new
motivation and goals, but our sinful tendencies remain. Therefore
we do require exhortation, rebuke, and discipline—and the Bible
is filled with it. The prophet Amos would have scorned the notion
that the Jews of his day were essentially a cooperative people
needing only a loving environment for their real selves to blossom
with love and good deeds. The Bible instructs us to "stimulate"
each other to greater love and better behavior (Heb. 10:24).
Passively accepting people where they are until they get around to
godly living is not a biblical strategy for encouragement.

Encouragement, therefore, must not be defined as either
rigorous exhortation or accepting warmth. Both will be involved in
the work of encouragement, but neither gets at the essence of what

encouragement is. Encouragement depends on loving motivation in the encourager as well as wisdom to discern the needs of the other person accurately. The actual words may be admonishing, rebuking, correcting, reproving, instructing, explaining, sympathizing, reflecting, affirming, or self-disclosing. If the motive is love and the target is fear, the words will be encouraging.

When that godly elder spoke to the young man who had just stuttered his way through a heretical prayer, his words arose out of loving concern and reflected an awareness of the young man's self-doubt. The result was encouragement.

Because I recognized an embarrassed woman's fear of looking foolish in Sunday school, simple words of greeting were encouraging.

Notice this: words aimed at fear do not necessarily speak openly about fear, but they always are spoken by someone who is conscious of the other's fear. I *am not* advocating that every encouraging sentence include a statement about fear; I *am* insisting that every encouraging sentence *reflect an awareness* that people are needy and fearful. Encouragers must constantly remind themselves that the people with whom they rub shoulders are facing problems in life which, but for the grace of God, are ultimately overwhelming. It is this conscious awareness that can give encouraging power to even the most trivial conversation.

One person can approach you and ask, "How are you?" and you respond casually, "Fine, thanks." The brief interchange is pleasant, innocuous, and soon forgotten. The event is no more significant than the bank teller's perfunctory "Have a good day" after you have deposited your weekly paycheck. Yet another person can greet you with the very same question and something in you responds at a deeper level as you say "Fine, thanks." You sense a certain eagerness in your answer; the moment is somehow meaningful. You walk away with a slightly more positive attitude, a little spring in your step.

Identical words—same question, same answer—but one interchange was commonplace and routinely dull, the other alive and heartwarming. Why the difference? The answer is as profound as it is simple. The first question moved from a layer to a layer, from a self-serving motive to an external part of your personality. The second went from love to fear, from a heart of ministry to a person who was accurately perceived as both valuable and in some way struggling.

The ministry of encouragement requires that the encourager have some awareness of what is happening inside people and that he speak words which reflect a genuine regard for others as valuable. The effect of encouragement is to stimulate the hope that solutions exist for every problem and that, seen from an eternal perspective, life does make sense. The hope stirs people to greater love and more good deeds and perseverance in godly living, despite fatigue and temptations. The point is important: *Encouragement is not a technique to be mastered; it is a sensitivity to people and a confidence in God that must be nourished and demonstrated.*

Words aimed at fear bring encouragement. Words aimed at layers generate pressure. When someone communicates that he understands my struggles or at least is sincerely trying to, and when his words reflect an awareness of what I feel, I am exposed. And exposure is what I fear. The whole system of layers has been designed to protect me from exposure. But when I stand emotionally naked before a discerning friend and then hear words that regard me as valuable, I am deeply encouraged. I have been seen as I am and still there is hope. The x-ray has been taken, the doctor has studied the pictures, he has faced the truth of my condition— and he smiles. Surgery may be required, painful recuperation may follow, but I will live.

The perfect example of encouragement is found, not surprisingly, in our relationship with Christ. The Lord Jesus declares us sinners and exposes us in all our filth. The diagnosis is worse than we feared: "Nothing good dwells in me, that is, in my flesh" (Rom. 7:18). We cringe in His presence, afraid to look into what we are certain will be an angry face. As we await the pronouncement of our well-deserved rejection, we hear words that dance in our minds, words so unexpected that we blink in astonishment. We listen again. We dare to look. Then we see His warm, loving smile and we hear Him repeat again, this time laughing gently at our surprise, "I don't condemn you. I forgive you. I love you and I want you to be a part of my eternal plan to spread the good news of acceptance and love." And I am eternally encouraged. He has spoken from His love to my fear.

God's perfect love casts out all fear. Our imperfect love—a poor, hopefully improving, but still feeble imitation of His love— can reduce fear. People will be encouraged as their fear is exposed through discernment and softened by love. The ministry of encouragement is speaking words that are prompted by love and directed toward fear.

SUMMARY

Words that encourage are motivated by the speaker's love and directed toward the hearer's fear.

Words motivated by the speaker's fear (that is, words spoken from a layer) and directed to the hearer's defensive patterns (or layers) generate pressure. They do not encourage.

To speak from love, encouragers must be willing to endure what they fear—the loss of relationship with others—in confidence that although all may forsake them, Christ never will.

Depending on Christ alone for relationship, encouragers must stay aware that people are both valuable and fearful. With this awareness reflected in all that they say, their words will be encouraging.

9
Encouragement: The Context for Change

Sometime ago I was in a discussion with other Christian counselors that centered on the important question, What really changes people? All of us were evangelicals committed to measuring our thinking by the norm of Scripture, and we agreed that the Holy Spirit is the final and indispensable agent of change. No meaningful movement toward godly wholeness is possible without His work.

Our concern, however, went beyond this core consensus. We wondered what we as counselors possess that has the power to make real impact. What do counselors have to offer that really is helpful? Is it our insight into human personality, our specialized verbal techniques, our ability to communicate empathic accep-tance, our powers of persuasion, our awareness of psychological issues, or our knowledge about how to live effectively? Dentists have the skills needed to restore a damaged tooth. What do counselors have?

The responses to the question fell into two main categories. One group felt that the central ingredient in counseling is the *relationship* between counselor and the person being counseled. Genuine care expressed through empathic understanding and discerning interaction would facilitate the sort of change Christian counselors want to promote.

The second group expressed a radically different view, although at first glance it might appear to be merely a shift in emphasis. According to this line of thought, the effective agent of change is not relationship but *clearly and authoritatively presented truth.* The counselor's job is to identify deviations from truth in the person's understanding and behavior and then present the violated truth in a way that demands response—either obedience or rebellion.

I felt uneasy about both positions, and it occurred to me that perhaps there was happy complementarity between them. I could think of enough Scripture about love and acceptance to keep me interested in the first view, but the biblical emphasis on obedience to truth required that I hang onto the second position as well. Continued reflection led me to the idea that maybe change takes place when *truth is presented in relationship.* Perhaps a relationship of deep regard and empathic concern is the *context* for change, creating an atmosphere in which the truth of God can be heard nondefensively and thus penetrate more deeply.

The two qualities—relationship and truth—go hand in hand, much like a cup and coffee. One without the other has little value. A focus on relationship without an equally insistent focus on truth results in undirected involvement. People who feel the warmth of a counselor may report that they feel better, and some of their problems may lessen; but it will be hard to ascertain whether the improvement reflects real movement toward Christian maturity.

On the other hand, the presentation of truth without a discerning awareness of people's hunger for relationship and identity may do nothing more than crowd people into a legalistic box. Behavior may change, but the inward reality will likely be pressured conformity with no experience of the liberty and love of Christ. Relationship without truth leads to shallow sentimentality. Truth without relationship generates pressure, then friction, and eventually disillusionment or pride.

We need both relationship and truth. Our counseling offices need both. Our families need both. Our churches need both. The most effective strategy for promoting substantial movement toward true godliness is to present truth in the context of relationship. Relationship cuts holes through defensive layers by reducing the core fear, thereby opening people up to truth. Biblical concepts and principles can then reach into the nerve center of the personality, displacing fear and stimulating conviction, repentance, and faith in a loving, holy God.

If the work of the teacher is to present truth clearly, then the work of the body is to develop relationship through the ministry of encouragement. Too often, teachers are exhorting unencouraged people to change. These people may change, but only superficially. They regularly attend the meetings of the church, they get up early for morning devotions, and they learn to share their faith with others. But something is missing. They rarely catch the quiet excitement of what it means to be pressing on to glory. Presenting truth to unencouraged Christians in our churches does little to promote biblical Christianity.

But churches that de-emphasize the teaching of God's Word in favor of "living out the truth of God's love in fulfilling, affirming relationships" fare no better. One cannot *experience* truth without first *knowing* truth. Concentrating on just portions of truth to the neglect of the full range and depth of biblical revelation will not promote strong, mature Christian character. What may appear to be spiritual growth will in reality be little more than emotional highs that will collapse under testing.

If we are to have both truth and relationship, we must envision churches that present truth to people who are enjoying fear-reducing relationships and are encouraging one another. Consider the effect that encouragement could have in the life of a local church. What happens when truth is presented—from the pulpit, in Sunday School, through Bible studies, at special conferences and seminars—to an *unencouraged congregation* versus an *encouraged congregation?*

TRUTH TO AN UNENCOURAGED CONGREGATION

"I wish his sermons were more practical" is a familiar complaint heard in parking lots after Sunday morning services. "The pastor talks about things which are of no real help to me at all. I wonder if he has any idea what life is like for an average person?" And then, as the complaints filter back to the pastor, the congregation must endure his efforts to be more relevant.

Too often, the sermons that get labeled "relevant" speak less of God than of people. Interesting stories replace solid exegesis, and eloquent delivery takes the place of spiritual power. Strong teaching that unearths the hidden treasures of Scripture is sacrificed to the need for reaching people where they live. Sermon preparation becomes a scrutinizing of "what people need" instead of a search for "what God says." And the pastor edges dangerously close to telling people only what they want to hear.

When people listen from behind layers, they will not be moved by truth. Their purpose in attending church is not to find

help in growth toward Christian maturity, but to continue in a
protected life of comfort. Biblical truth is not relevant to someone
with that goal any more than directions to Alaska are helpful to a
traveler en route to Florida. Layered people are predisposed to
maintain some degree of personal comfort. To do so they must
scrupulously avoid self-examination in the light of biblical truth. In
the face of biblical preaching, the complaints begin: "The sermons
really don't do much for me."

The pastor responds to the complaints by concluding that
expository preaching doesn't change lives. He sees attendance
dwindling when he emphasizes serious Bible study, and he
mistakenly determines that he is merely filling people's minds with
facts rather than life-giving truth. So he changes his approach to
preaching. But the problem may lie not with the preaching. It may
be the listening that's faulty. Perhaps the real problem is that the
majority of the congregation are unencouraged people, safely shut
in behind their layers and protected from sensing vital truth.

When sermons are criticized as "irrelevant," it does no good
to shift from biblical preaching to "meeting needs." If the
preaching is biblical, it *is* relevant. But if biblical preaching *seems*
irrelevant, then perhaps people are listening from behind their
layers.

Pastors who have scrapped a scriptural teaching focus in their
preaching in favor of a dynamic personal style should reconsider.
When preachers announce a biblical text and then present a lively
talk that never grapples with the text, they fail in their calling.
They do well to return to biblical preaching and at the same time
take a hard look at their congregation. Is encouragement being
practiced? Is it understood? Are the saints actively concerned with
encouraging one another?

The proper response to complaints of irrelevancy is to help
people change their motivation from self-protective manipulation
to Christ-exalting ministry. This change can be facilitated by
encouragement. Without the work of encouragement, people will
continue to listen from behind their layers and truth will not get
through.

When an unencouraged person listens to the truth of God,
one of two things will happen. Either (1) the biblical principles
will not get through his layers, or (2) they will strengthen his fear
and thus thicken his layers. These alternatives are demonstrated in
the experiences of Vic and Ralph.

Vic is a successful businessman, a three-piece-suit and dinner-at-the-club kind of man, personable and socially at ease in most public situations. He was raised in a middle-income home with a father who never found the formula for gaining wealth and knew the sting of a limited income. Vic's parents endured a tolerable marriage interrupted frequently by arguments over money. Vic remembers hearing a steady flow of complaints from his mother about having to stretch her household allowance farther than it could go.

But Vic is also feeling pressure. Beneath the look of confidence lies deep fear: "I have to be more successful than dad or I'll be unhappy just like him." Single-minded zeal to seek first his kingdom resulted in a comfortable income, a lovely home in a fairly prestigious neighborhood, two fashionable cars, membership in the country club, and frequent cocktails before dinner to celebrate his emancipation from middle-class Christianity into the good life of self-sufficiency and success.

Because Vic is a professing Christian, part of his success package includes church attendance, prayer before mealtimes, and occasional family devotions. But all these things serve to hide, even from himself, the deep sense of inadequacy that drives him toward the visible reminders of success. His fear is deep, his layers thick.

Most people at the church like Vic. He is a pleasant person to know. But no one *really* knows him; no one ever gets close enough to see what he's really like. His fears remain conveniently shielded from view, so well hidden that not even he is aware that his purpose in living is to prove a point and reduce a fear.

Because no one understands him, no one really encourages Vic. Because fear continues to quietly dominate his life, his layers stay firmly in place, thickened to the point that he will let nothing puncture his false sense of security. Vic is blind to his own spiritual poverty.

The prophet Hosea painted a similar picture to describe the condition of an apostate Jewish nation in his day: "Gray hairs also are sprinkled on him, yet he does not know it" (Hos. 7:9). Signs of moral aging were visible, but the people thought they were in prime spiritual health. Hosea decried the fact that the signs of *moral* degeneracy which should be plainly visible are often not seen by the people affected.

The point of the analogy is that it is not natural to be unaware of the evidence of age. When I encounter friends whom I have not seen for years, I often receive comments like, "You've put on a little weight, I see" or "Quite a bit of new gray hair around the temples." Do they suppose I hadn't noticed? Sometimes I feel tempted to enjoy sinful revenge and say, "You're really quite tubby yourself, and your face has many more wrinkles than I recall." But I would be adding nothing to their awareness as they have added nothing to mine. It is natural to see all too clearly the evidence of physical decline.

Yet people are afraid to look at themselves honestly, to see marks of moral decline, to pry beneath the layers and expose greed, fear, and pride. Many of us have found a comfort zone, and we want no one meddling with it. I think there are many Vics singing in church choirs and serving on church boards. They are blinded to the light of biblical truth no matter how sensitively presented. Many years' practice at tuning out threats of confrontation has made the process of denial almost automatic. Vic is able to sit through sermons without feeling more than a twinge of conviction. He is complacent, and his complacency is strengthened with every selective disregard for truth.

Ralph is different. He is visibly insecure, a borderline white-collar worker, not especially talented, married to a woman of no special talent, the father of ordinary kids who make C's and drop footballs during gym class, a man whose leisure time is divided between television and yardwork. Ralph has not been blessed with the tools to develop all the effective layers that can shield him from his fear of being useless and unimportant. His layers, unlike Vic's, leave him short of complacency. The best he can do is to numb his pain with TV and the absence of reflective thinking.

When Ralph shows up in the church membership class, no one is excited about it. While Vic is shaking hands and chatting sociably, Ralph takes four of five minutes to stir his sugared coffee, hoping to disguise his feelings of isolation. As Ralph listens to the pastor remind his listeners that Christian people should be excited about God, a wave of shoulder-shrugging emptiness sweeps over him. He put his faith in Christ at a youth rally when he was sixteen years old, but he has never experienced much of the abundance he walked down the aisle to find. And now as he listens to a recitation of what he should do and feel, he grudgingly promises God that he will read his Bible more faithfully and provide spiritual leadership for his family.

And he tries, motivated by persistent pressure to be what he should be. But this effort proves no more fruitful than the dozen earlier rededications. It simply does not work. He is a "nobody" and nothing will change that brute fact. Perhaps he endures for a while, hoping that continued well-doing will yield a harvest. Eventually he quits. He rebels against the oppressive system that points an accusing finger at his spiritual stupor without providing a workable plan for change.

He turns to drinking a little more and to stopping occasionally at an adult bookstore. It may be wrong, but it affords at least some relief, a lift that he can feel, something that church has never offered. Church attendance becomes spotty, domestic arguments increase, and Ralph's wife becomes concerned. She shares her worry with the adult Sunday school teacher, and his response is, "I wish there were something the church could do. Some folks just don't want to go God's way. All we can do is pray." And the church writes him off.

Vic and Ralph represent two end points on a continuum of people whose layers are more or less successful. The more effective the layer, the greater the likelihood that truth will generate complacency. The less effective the layer, the greater the likelihood that truth will promote despair and rebellion. An unencouraged congregation often becomes either blindly complacent—though often spiritual-looking—or disinterested.

TRUTH TO AN ENCOURAGED CONGREGATION

There is powerful potential in encouragement. Consider how life could be different for Vic and Ralph if someone were to invest the time needed to treat them meaningfully instead of superficially.

A discerning believer recognizes that Vic is a layered person. As part of his commitment to Christ and His body, he determines to minister to Vic. Through showing genuine love, a relationship develops in which the encourager recognizes that his primary purpose is to reduce fear, not to change layers. He does not quickly confront Vic about his spiritual immaturity and wrong priorities.

As the relationship deepens, Vic shares a bit more of himself which the perceptive encourager sees as the visible tip of Vic's iceberg of fear. He puts the fear into words and says, "Vic, it's really important to you to make money and to display the evidence of your prosperity. I wonder if you would have trouble seeing yourself as a valuable person if you didn't have money."

Note the two important elements in this encouraging sentence: (1) The fear is put into words that are understandable to the fearful person; and (2) the words communicate genuine acceptance of the other as a valuable (though perhaps wrong) person. There is *exposure without rejection.* That defines encouragement.

The result is that Vic's fear reduces. Gradually, even imperceptibly, his attachment to the symbols of success weakens. His layers develop holes, providing opportunity for the Spirit of Truth to reach inside him. Then, as he sits under biblical teaching, Vic begins to experience a desire to pursue God. He chooses— much as a child chooses to eat an ice cream cone—to spend less time at the club and more time in church activities. Without the effects of encouragement, biblical exhortation may drive Vic to attend church more often, but he will do it the way children eat carrots: dutifully and reluctantly. But with encouragement, the truth of God motivates in positive ways. Vic is growing.

Let us assume that Ralph was also befriended. One encouraging member of the body made a skillfull attempt to get close to Ralph in the hope of affirming his value as a person in spite of his lackluster circumstances. And Ralph responds. He smiles appreciatively when the encourager approaches him and agrees to meet for coffee after the evening service.

Despite the faithful encouraging efforts, however, Ralph slowly drifts away from spiritual things. Encouraging comments provoke a less eager smile, invitations for coffee are more often declined, church and Bible study attendance becomes more irregular, and the encourager feels somewhat discouraged. What has happened? Did encouragement fail to reduce the fear and to penetrate the layers?

The problem is that people are not only fearful but stubborn. The heart of man is desperately wicked. People are determined to handle life without believing God and kneeling before Him. Ralph's problem goes beyond just dealing with his layers. His fear is not the only obstacle to personal growth. Ralph's sinful heart simply refuses to believe God, and so Ralph falls away. The reason for his disinterest cannot be traced to a failure in encouragement.

CONCLUSION

When the truth of God is presented well to an *unencouraged congregation,* it will generally promote either *complacency* or *intimidation.* Complacent people may appear to be spiritual, especially in churches that define success in terms of size, building projects, and program diversity. Intimidated people may conform to whatever standards of spirituality are imposed on them (participation in fund-raising campaigns, attendance at the Sunday evening service, having a regular if mechanical quiet time, etc.). Or the fearful who are intimidated may simply quit trying to measure up and become (at least in the minds of the intimidators) rebellious or disinterested in Christian growth.

When the truth of God is presented well to an *encouraged congregation,* it will generally promote either *real growth* or *real rebellion.* Ironically, a healthy church is full of people who either grow or rebel. And to be healthy, *a church must present truth in the context of encouraging relationships.*

SUMMARY

Truth presented to people who are not involved in encouraging relationships will generally not realize its potential to change lives, humanly speaking.

Warm, affirming relationships that neglect the truth of biblical directives may promote happy feelings and improved self-images, but they do not promote godly character.

Maximum growth in Christian maturity occurs when truth is presented in the context of relationships.

LAYER

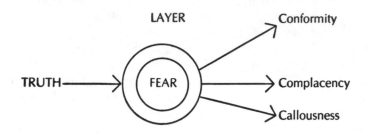

10

Opportunities for Encouragement

Meeting together with fellow Christians is intended to provide us with opportunities to meaningfully encourage one another. This is the point of the key text in this book, Hebrews 10:24–25: "And let us consider how to stimulate one another to love and good deeds, not forsaking our own assembling together, as is the habit of some, but encouraging one another; and all the more, as you see the day drawing near."

Too often, however, our fellowship is routine and trivial—warm enough perhaps, but not richly encouraging. Christians in conversation sometimes represent nothing more than self-interested, anxious people bumping politely into each other's layers. Nothing is very encouraging in that.

Happily, the reality of our experience is often better. Church attendance or participation in a midweek Bible study sometimes does have significant impact on our lives. As I write, I am enjoying the warm afterglow of an especially good time spent in a church I visited during a trip. The people were friendly, the pastor's sermon drew me toward the Lord with its insightful simplicity, and a gracious couple invited me to Sunday dinner. I was encouraged to pursue the path of obedience more fervently. At times like these, the words of the song "What a thrill that I feel when I get together with God's wonderful people" echo my sentiments.

Sometimes, however, things go differently. Handshakes seem insincere, the sermon comes across like a parental scolding, the faraway look of wistful piety effected by the soloist appears contrived and theatric, kids slouch rebelliously in their seats and grudgingly respond to parents' pinches by sitting up halfway—and we are neither encouraged nor encouraging. Driving to church is sometimes no more appealing than a trip to the dentist.

It will do no good to pretend that church services are always exciting times of worship, learning, and fellowship. Christians—including pastors, Sunday school teachers, and ushers—can be irritating, selfish, petty, dishonest, scheming, silly, cold, insensitive, dull, and arrogant. And yet we are expected to find opportunities to encourage one another when we get together with "God's wonderful people." How? When our conversations consist of pointless chatter, sour-faced grumbling, and frivolous banalities, how are we to find opportunity for slipping in encouraging words?

To address this question practically, I must develop two points:

1. Opportunities for encouragement will go unrecognized unless we consciously choose the goal of ministry as we talk with people;

2. Hidden opportunities for encouragement will surface as we express sensitive recognition of potential needs.

THE GOAL OF MINISTRY

Much of our discussion so far has emphasized the need to maintain a single-minded motivation as we talk to people. We are actively to pursue the purpose of ministering to one another. The problem, of course, is that this ideal is far easier to discuss than to practice. My concern is to bring the idea of the goal of ministry down to a level where we can do something with it next Sunday morning.

Picture the mind as a cassette tape recorder that is always running. Sometimes we can hear the mental tape we are playing; at other times we can't. On occasion, the volume is turned so high that our own thoughts thoroughly consume our awareness, blocking out input from any source outside ourselves. When that happens, we lose contact with reality. Usually, however, we maintain the volume of our thinking tape at a level just beyond the range of our conscious attention. In other words, people typically pay little attention to what they are thinking at any given moment

If I were to approach someone filing out of church and abruptly ask him, "What are you saying to yourself right now?" the immediate response would very likely be a confused stammer: "Uh, I don't know, I wasn't thinking much of anything." Yet he *was* thinking something. Our minds are rarely empty. The tape recorder is *always* playing a set of sentences. And when we concentrate on it, we become aware of at least some of the words on that tape.

Though we may not be consciously aware of what we are telling ourselves at every given moment, the words that fill our minds control much of what we do and feel. Much of our behavior is a direct product of what we are thinking unconsciously. Therefore it is important to tune in to our thinking, to hear what we are telling ourselves, and to actively replace sentences that reflect *wrong* goals and lead to *selfish* behavior with sentences that reflect *right* goals and lead to *selfless* behavior.

As an example, consider what might be happening at an evangelical church on a Sunday morning. Hundreds of people file into a church building from the parking lot. Parents point children toward their Sunday school classrooms, friends exchange cheery greetings, women smoothe their hair, and men straighten their ties: Christians are assembling themselves together.

Suppose a special microphone were wired to pick up the sentences playing just at or below awareness level in the mental tape recorders of all these people. If we were eavesdropping, what might we hear?

> "Oh, no! There's Fred pulling up in his car. If he sees me, he'll ask me for that committee report I haven't done yet. I'd better move inside quickly and get seated."

> "I wish my husband weren't away on that business trip. It's really uncomfortable coming to church without him. Well, I'll just sit in the back and leave as soon as the service is over."

> "I sure hope the preaching is better than it's been the last few weeks."

> "This should be a really good day. No work that needs to be done. I like our church and the football game is on TV at 3 this afternoon. That gives me time to take the family out to dinner and still be home for the kickoff. I really like being a Christian."

> "I wonder if I should keep coming to this church. I really haven't made any friends and the sermons don't do much for me. Well I'll keep praying about it and see how it goes today."

"Look at that happy young family. It really hurts when I realize my kids are grown, gone, unsaved, and mixed-up. Boy, I wish I could have a few years back. Well I can't start crying now. C'mon, smile—here comes Nancy to say hello."

"People think of me as a pretty spiritually together person. I'll make a point to interact graciously and to respond in a biblical way to whatever happens."

With tapes like these playing quietly in the mental recorders of the gathering saints, the chances are slim that any real encouragement will take place during the time they spend together. The fact is, most of us do not come to church with any intention of providing encouragement. And the thoughts we think reflect that lack of intention.

Everything we say or do is moving toward a goal. As people we are teleological beings; that is, we are controlled by our purposes. If we want to change what we are doing, then we must first change what we are trying to accomplish. Broadly speaking, all our purposes can be sorted into two categories: either we *manipulate* for our own self-enhancement or self-protection, or we *minister* for the glory of God and the well-being of others. The words we say to ourselves, whether we are aware of them or not, reflect (and in some sense determine) the goals we pursue. For example, lonely people often pursue the goal of companionship. Therefore their tapes have to do with hoping for friendliness, avoiding rejection, or evaluating their social impact. They are not looking for opportunities to encourage. Accordingly, they don't find them.

We will encourage no one until we deliberately attend to our thoughts, identify tapes that indicate goals other than encouragement, and replace them with new mental tapes that reflect the purpose of ministry. The writer to the Hebrews specifically instructs us to *consider* how to encourage one another (Heb. 10:24-25). We are to turn our attention to the matter of encouragement consciously, intentionally, and with mental discipline.

Think what would happen if just ten believers in any given church deliberately chose to play a tape such as "I know many people are burdened and hurting. To whom can I speak with words of love and concern?" The assembly of which they were a part would begin to experience the reality of encouragement.

When the idea first became clear to me that every word I utter should be governed by the motive of ministry, I struggled to build a new mental tape library. When I arrived home from work every evening, I remained in my car for a few minutes and repeated to myself, "My goal as I walk through the front door is to minister to my family. I sure hope I'm greeted by a happy wife, delightful kids, and a working refrigerator, but no matter what I discover inside, my purpose is to minister in love to my family."

For many men, there are few moments more fearful than returning home after a day's work. As they stumble wearily through the front door, their mental tape recorders often play words like "I hope the hamster didn't fall in the toilet again" or "If my wife gripes about her day after the one I've just had, I think I'll walk out." Thoughts of this sort tempt husbands to wrap themselves in protective layers of bored silence, cold retreat, or absorption in the TV or newspaper.

Self-protective manipulation comes naturally; servant-like ministry doesn't. The attitude of ministry requires careful cultivation. Unless we diligently attend to our thinking and choose to adopt the goal of ministry by playing the right mental tapes, we will drift inevitably into layer-to-layer fellowship. If meeting together with brothers and sisters in Christ is to become a time of encouragement, the first requirement is that we make it our goal to encourage.

VERBAL SENSITIVITY TO NEEDS

If our goal is to minister, we will be actively looking for opportunities to encourage. But how do we recognize them? What are we to do? Are we to approach a prospective person to be encouraged, lay a hand meaningfully on his shoulder, and with compassionate eyes say, "Hi, I'm here to encourage you"? Exactly how do we go about this task of finding and responding to opportunities for encouragement?

Encouragement occurs most effectively when opportunities are *seized* rather than created. It is a mistake to regard encouragement as a vividly dramatic interchange full of rich emotional display. Certainly occasions like that happen, and they can be meaningful. But encouragement more often takes place during what appears to be very ordinary conversation. A few words are spoken that if overheard may seem uneventful. But something happens: a person is encouraged. Remember, the power of encouragement does not lie primarily in the words; it lies in the motivation behind the words. If we attend to commonplace interactions with a sensitive ear, a ministry-motivated mind, and a loving heart, we will not lack for opportunities to encourage. Nevertheless, how do we find them?

In any group of people a fair number will be wrestling with immediate concerns of varying degrees of severity: guilt over sexual fantasies, anxiety about an upcoming doctor's appointment, fatigue from a demanding schedule, loneliness aggravated by a best friend's recent relocation, money worries, resentment toward a rejecting spouse, frustration with parents who freely dispense advice—the list is endless. Other people, whose minds may not be currently focusing on a problem, are still facing concerns that could soon become pressing.

Very few of us, however, openly publicize our burdens. And that, I suppose, is just as well. Emotional exhibitionists who regard the display of neurosis as a virtue make a fetish out of becoming vulnerably open. Christian fellowship is not designed to be a forum for revealing personal problems; rather, it is an opportunity to share with others the relevance of Christ's life to ours. This does require self-disclosure and openness, not as an end in itself, but as a means to the end of knowing Christ more fully.

But most of us tend to disguise our concerns behind socially acceptable masks. We keep these masks in place to avoid the criticism and disapproval we fear would follow the exposure of what we really feel. Yet the layers do more than *protect*; they also *isolate*. Soon we feel cut off from the relationship our natures desire. Our defenses not only block out rejection, but also remove us from the reach of love. From behind our layers, we long to be known and accepted. So we drop subtle clues about what is happening inside, looking for some sign that our listener is attentive, sensitive, and accepting. Like a timid swimmer dipping his toe in the water to see if the temperature is inviting, we reveal enough of ourselves to test the warmth of our listener's attitude.

"How are you?" a friend might casually inquire. The truth is that my head is pounding, the kids bickered all the way to church, and one of my parents is evidencing frightening medical symptoms. But I answer, "Oh, pretty good, I guess—all things considering."

Perhaps my friend responds, "Yea, it takes a lot to stay on top these days. Hey, good to see you!" *He has missed an opportunity to encourage.* The opportunity was not advertised in lights, but still it was there. My offhand reply was a veiled invitation to inquire further—veiled because I was not at all sure that my friend was really interested in how I feel. Had he been actively looking for an opportunity to encourage, he might have realized that "Oh, pretty good, I guess—all things considering" is a very different response from "Hey, really good! How are things with you?" The tentative wording was designed to convey a message that if my friend wanted to provide encouragement, I was eager and open to receiving it.

The point can be summarized in a phrase: encouragers must develop the skill of *listening beneath words.* Words often communicate not only an open, visible message but also a subtle, hidden message. And hidden messages need to be heard.

Still, an important caution is in order: *not every sentence is communicating a disguised need.* There is nothing less encouraging than a would-be encourager stalking victims by reading problems into every word.

> "How are you doing?"
>
> "Fine, thanks."
>
> "'Fine?' I wonder if you mean that. How are you *really* doing?"

Although there is a clear danger of seeing deep hurts in every casual encounter, there is a greater danger in failing to recognize legitimate concerns hidden under chitchat. Consider the skill of listening beneath words.

After church one Sunday morning, a friend remarks, "That really wasn't much of a sermon today." What are the possible messages lurking underneath his comment? He might mean nothing more than what he said—perhaps the sermon was mediocre. But what more might be concealed in those words? Here are some possibilities:

> "The sermon struck a nerve, but I don't want to deal with the conviction."
>
> "I have a personal grudge against the pastor. I wouldn't appreciate anything he said."
>
> "I wish I were given a chance to teach or preach. I think it would be rewarding to be up front."
>
> "I'm struggling with problems that the pastor never talks about. It's hard to appreciate a sermon on Elijah's battle with Baal's priests when you're seriously considering a divorce."

A person committed to the ministry of encouragement must *listen.* Rather than thinking through his response while the other speaks, he will be listening. Active listening requires concentrated effort. It notices facial grimaces, slumped shoulders, quiet sighs, lifeless tones of voice, and moist eyes. The comment "That really wasn't much of a sermon today" should be a stimulus for careful thought.

Perhaps this is the prayed-for opportunity to encourage. Perhaps not. If step one is to attend to the possibility of hidden messages, what is step two? What should an encourager say when he suspects that someone is communicating a veiled concern?

Sensitive listeners respond to comments with *words that convey an interest in hearing more*, sentences that open the door to information. Words that open doors transmit two messages:

1. "I am interested in whatever you have to say."
2. "I will accept you regardless of what you say."

In response to the remark "That really wasn't much of a sermon today," an encourager might offer one of these door-openers:

"What are your thoughts?"
"I'd like to hear what you mean."
"Oh?"
"Not much?"
"Didn't do much for you, huh?"

Too often, people respond with *door closers* rather than *door openers*. Door closers—words that shut off any hope of further, deeper sharing—convey a lack of sensitive interest in what may be happening in the other person. They also carry a hint of criticism that threatens the possibility of rejection. Door closers discourage further discussion by communicating insensitivity and critical disinterest. They thwart the process of encouragement by increasing fear of rejection and aloneness.

Conversations between Christians should be marked by compassionate sensitivity. We must regard people as more than collections of chemicals that come together during gestation and fall apart at death. People are *persons*, beings who bear the image of God; people are fallen but valuable. We rub shoulders every day with unique beings whose destiny is awesome—either eternal glory or everlasting despair.

To put the matter plainly, people are worth listening to. A cup of water offered to the least of God's creatures is a noteworthy deed. Our calling and privilege is to involve ourselves in other people's lives with the purpose of stimulating them to love and good deeds. When our *goal is ministry* and when we verbally express *sensitivity to needs* by listening underneath words and responding with door openers, we will begin to recognize the encouragement opportunities that abound whenever Christians assemble together.

SUMMARY

When Christians assemble, there are countless opportunities to encourage one another, but they often go unrecognized.

To recognize an opportunity to encourage someone, people must meet two conditions: (1) They must consciously remind themselves, as they interact with others, that their goal is to encourage; (2) They must realize that people don't normally reveal their concerns openly. More often, they drop hints that things are not as they should be. When an encourager suspects that a brother or sister is sharing a disguised need, he must respond with sensitivity.

Door openers convey an accepting interest in whatever the other wants to say; door closers convey a bored or critical indifference to whatever may be troubling the other.

11
Responding to Opportunities

If we remind ourselves to remain alert for opportunities, and if we respond with door openers to possible messages hidden beneath words, then we will encounter situations that beg for encouragement. There are so few real listeners that when someone does incline his ear to others, he will stumble regularly into people who need encouragement.

But sensitive listening creates an imposing problem. Suppose someone reacts to a door opener by actually opening the door. What is an encourager to do when someone drops his layer and reveals his struggles?

One sincere Christian man who enrolled in a course on encouragement put it this way: "I'm a little scared to go around opening doors. What would I do if someone laid something heavy on me like 'My marriage is falling apart' or 'My kid is on drugs' or 'I have a homosexual problem.' I wouldn't have the faintest idea what to say. I'm afraid I'd do more harm than good. Man, I don't know what to say when someone tells me he's a little depressed, let alone something big."

The concern is understandable, and it is one reason why people close more doors than they open. When we prompt someone to shed his layer and share an aspect of his life that was formerly hidden, what do we do next? The difficult part of surgery may not be cutting into the body. Although skill is required to make the incision without disfiguring or endangering the patient, the central work of surgery begins once the problem is uncovered. The surgeon's ability is most needed when the diseased organ lies exposed before him. In keeping with this analogy, our greatest need as encouragers is to know what to do when the verbal incision has been made and a need lies exposed before us.

Having used some examples of encouraging words in the previous chapter, I must state again that we do not learn to encourage by memorizing a list of phrases. There is no such list, at least none worth memorizing. Encouragement is not a technique based on selecting certain words; it is an attitude, a view of others as valuable with a commitment to treat them accordingly.

Encouragement does, however, require words. Therefore it is necessary to face the problem of choosing the right words to say. It may be helpful to approach the problem by defining a few *principles of encouragement*. If, as we speak to hurting people, we keep these principles in our minds and endeavor to speak consistently with them, our words will very likely have the power to encourage.

1. The essence of encouragement is exposure without rejection.

2. Understanding sometimes offers more encouragement than advice.

3. The more precise the understanding, the more encouraging the words.

PRINCIPLE 1: THE ESSENCE OF ENCOURAGEMENT IS EXPOSURE WITHOUT REJECTION

The central function of a layer is to protect. To come out from behind a layer means losing protection. The exposed person is in line to experience some form of rejection. Indifference, criticism, irritation, impatience, sarcasm, withdrawal, and disapproval are but a few of the many ways to reject someone as less than valuable. At the core of our beings we all fear rejection, whatever form it takes.

It is true that Christians are fully accepted by God because of Jesus' shed blood. For us, there is now no condemnation. But somehow we fail to grasp that God's acceptance makes anyone else's rejection no more devastating than a misplaced dollar would be to a millionaire. We foolishly believe that other people's acceptance represents a legitimate measure of our value. We fear the rejection of people and therefore hide from them.

With this understanding of people's fear, we can see that the strength of encouragement lies in its communication of acceptance to an exposed person. My wife often sees me standing behind a pulpit or seminar podium teaching others how to live for Christ; but she also has the opportunity to watch how I handle the frustration of a broken lawn mower or the trial of a heavy schedule. Better than anyone else, she knows how imperfectly I live what I preach. I am exposed in her presence—and accepted. I am exposed and accepted—and therefore encouraged.

When a staff member's poor attitude demands a corrective response, the senior pastor may need to speak words of admonition. As the staff member listens to an explanation of his error, he is exposed. He may continue to retreat behind layers of defensiveness, apology, or arrogance, but still, in some measure, he stands exposed. Whenever a person's weaknesses are visible to himself and another, there is opportunity for profound encouragement—or discouragement.

To provide encouragement, the pastor should take pains to convey confidence in the staff member's potential to change. And he should allow freedom for him to wrestle with the rebuke: "Let's talk this over next week after we both can spend time in prayer." If the rebuke is direct and gentle rather than vague or brutal, then the admonition may encourage.

If, however, the pastor's words reflect disgust, disappointment, impatience, or irritation, then no encouragement will occur. Encouragement depends fundamentally on *accepting* a person whose needs and faults lie exposed.

Sometimes encouragement may involve an almost comically trivial exposure. During a recent trip I discovered, much to my dismay, that the shower in my motel room was broken. I heard a maid bustling about in the hallway and mentioned my dilemma to her. With a sincere nod, she promised to report the matter to maintenance.

Several hours later, as I was returning to my room after addressing a conference, I chanced to walk by the same maid. She stopped folding towels long enough to look up and say, "I told the desk about your shower. If it isn't fixed by now, I think you should change rooms."

Her words, I noticed, generated a bit of warmth in me. I had exposed a need to her—hardly a significant one but still a need— and she had heard me. She had taken my problem seriously. Thinking back, I realized that I had expected her to do nothing, to react to my stated need with indifference Instead, she cared. Exposure with acceptance, even at this level, is encouraging.

PRINCIPLE 2: UNDERSTANDING IS SOMETIMES BETTER THAN ADVICE

When people make known a concern, most of us immediately feel pressure. "What do I say now? How can I help? I don't know what to tell him he should do." The pressure is *self-imposed.* We take it upon ourselves to solve the other person's problems, and then we feel the pressure of figuring out a solution.

Our mistake is to assume that the person who shares a problem is really asking us for a solution. A husband complaining to his wife about job tensions is rarely requesting that she come up with alternative employment possibilities or improved coping strategies. Rather, he is simply asking to be understood and accepted. "I hurt. Do you care?"

Yet wives (and husbands, when the situation is reversed) inevitably respond with "Maybe you ought to quit and look for a better job." Then they feel puzzled and confused when their attempt to help is met with an angry retort: "Sure, jobs are a dime a dozen. How can I pay the bills if I quit?"

Lost people need direction. Blind people need enlightening. Stubborn people need prodding. Clear instruction on how to handle life's problems is obviously necessary. But people are not only lost, blind, and stubborn; they are also scared. And scared people need patient, accepting understanding. Christians must grasp the apparently elusive truth that advice without understanding is not helpful. It is in fact a form of rejection.

Quick advice communicates disrespect and disinterest. The words *spoken* may be "I think that you should. . . ." The words *heard* may be "Your problem is simple. But you're too stupid to figure out a solution. So I'll tell you what to do."

The job of the encourager is to provide understanding and acceptance. Direct advice based on biblical teaching is a necessary part of helping someone who does not know what to do. But the unique work of encouragement is preparing people to take good advice more willingly by opening them up through acceptance. Encouragers do not need to feel the pressure of applying specific remedies to every problem. Perhaps another brother or sister in Christ, more experienced and knowledgeable in the Scriptures, should be called in to provide clear direction. The encourager must see the rich value of providing understanding.

Quiet listening, sensitive probing, clarifying inquiry, discerning restatement are a few ways to promote and convey understanding. These verbal strategies will be discussed in later chapters. But in them all, the message of the encourager is "I hear you, I want to hear more from you, and I believe you are a valuable human being."

PRINCIPLE 3: THE MORE PRECISE THE UNDERSTANDING, THE MORE ENCOURAGING THE WORDS

Encouragers must not only (1) provide for exposure without rejection and (2) seek to sensitively understand whatever a person may be saying, but (3) they must also speak words that promote awareness of a person's value. To do so, encouragers need to understand precisely what it is that makes a person valuable.

The Bible teaches that people are unique. We bear the image of God. Whatever else that image may encompass, it certainly includes the fact that people are capable of (1) entering into relationships of love and (2) engaging in activities with meaning. We are designed for relationship and meaningful activity. God had fellowship with Adam and Eve, and He assigned important work for them to do.

Because we are created, finite beings, we are dependent upon our infinite Creator for the resources we need to live full, whole lives. We therefore *need* relationship and we *need* meaning; we require both love and purpose. Or, in terms I have used in other books, people need *security* and *significance*. The security of enjoying a love that cannot be lost and the significance of pursuing activities with eternal consequence are available only through relationship to Christ.

The essential fear that is locked deep in the core of fallen people is the fear of insecurity (rejection) and insignificance (loss of value). If encouragers clearly understand that these two deep longings lie beneath people's layers of self-sufficiency, their words may reflect a greater understanding of people's fears.

Encouraging words identify the desire for relationship, penetrating beneath whatever layers are presented. A recently divorced woman told me that she knew God would see her through the unwelcome adjustment to single living. I sensed that her confidence was more contrived than genuine and, remembering how fervently people long for relationship, simply remarked, "Feeling lonely?"

She burst into tears and poured out her heart, expressing terrible fears that life would never be joyful again. Still reminding myself that she needed relationship, I simply listened, providing her with at least one person who accepted and cared about her. I then prayed with her and asked the Lord to bring a deep sense of His presence into her life.

Words that encourage take into account both the need for relationship and the need for meaning. All of us want to know we matter. We long to make an impact. It is difficult to leave a church fellowship after many years of active involvement and find that the gap created by our absence is quickly and painlessly filled. God designed us with the intention that we make a difference in our world. When we are aware of making a positive impact, we feel good.

It follows that an excellent way to encourage people is to let them know of the difference they have made in other people's lives, ours included. Statements like "Your smile really cheers me up" or "The way you treat your kids has been a super example for me to follow" or "The consistency of your life has helped me believe that the Christian life can really work" can be most encouraging.

Encouragers will be sensitive to ways in which they can pick up on the basic needs and say something that can bring hope to a person who otherwise might despair of ever experiencing the security and significance available in Christ. A precise understanding of people's needs can assist the encourager to be more encouraging.

SUMMARY

People are reluctant to involve themselves in others' lives by opening conversational doors. One reason for this reluctance is an understandable fear that they will not know what to say if another opens the door and reveals a personal struggle.

This fear is best understood as the result of self-imposed pressure to offer solutions to every stated problem. But such pressure reflects a faulty understanding of the nature of encouragement.

Encouragement is a process that reflects the operation of three principles:

1. Words that encourage express acceptance in the presence of an exposed need or problem.

2. Premature advice (advice given before the problem is understood) communicates disrespect for the person and his problem. The serious effort to understand (not solve) a problem is central to the work of encouragement.

3. Because the basic fear of people involves a fear of losing what they need—love and purpose—encouraging words convey both acceptance and an awareness of impact made by the person on his world.

12
Techniques of
Encouragement: I

There are very real obstacles that must be overcome if we are to become truly encouraging people. Two of these have been discussed in earlier chapters: manipulation and layers. If we want to encourage we must first learn to identify and then actively challenge our natural motivation to *use* others.

The realization that motives are not always pure is enough to stop many people in their tracks. I spoke to a middle-aged Christian lady whose son was about to marry an older woman with two children. She pleaded with me to persuade him that he was making an awful decision. As I probed the relationship between mother and son, I found that for fifteen years she had maneuvered her son into his profession, house, car, and dating relationships. She was now at her wits' end because she realized that in the most important battle—the choice of her son's wife—she had lost control. In working with her, my objective was to help her give up the role of guardian angel and learn the very different role of mother.

Her response was angry and adamant: "I've *never* done anything that was not for his good." She could not recognize the manipulative goal behind her behavior, because she was blinded by a combination of twisted love, fear, and jealous pride. The fine line between *concern* and *control* is difficult to recognize. Manipulation can look like ministry.

A second obstacle hindering us from developing into effective

---

Chapters 12 and 13 are written by Dan Allender.

encouragers is the habit of living behind self-protective layers. Remember that a layer is a protective shield enabling us to quiet our fears of insecurity and insignificance while projecting a veneer of confidence. These layers help us to interact comfortably with each other by keeping our distance. The church comedian, the serious theologian, the signs-of-the-times enthusiast, the sweet socializer, and the shy wallflower may all be playing roles that enable them to comfortably control their environment from behind protective layers.

Because it is crucial to understand this concept of layers, we should consider an example in which the defensive function of a layer is clearly apparent. When she was fifteen months old, our daughter Anna was caught red-handed pulling the refrigerator molding off its base. Her response was to shift attention abruptly away from her misdemeanor by smiling brightly and shouting, "Hi, Daddy! Hi, Daddy!" and then laughing hysterically. A born comic? No, just an inherently self-sufficient little girl who had learned an effective way of postponing or reducing unpleasant consequences by putting on the layer of comedy. She has undoubtedly learned some of her techniques from her layered father, because he also wants to avert adverse consequences and hide from the fear of personal inadequacy. Two of my favorite techniques might be called "blustering bravado" and "assertive avoidance."

Here is another personal example. A fluorescent light once burned out in our kitchen. For the first night, dinner by candlelight seemed like an innovative and romantic remedy. After a week passed, the novelty of burning candles had understandably lost its charm to my wife. In spite of limited knowledge about sophisticated machinery like fluorescent lights, I bravely purchased a new light, put it in, turned on the switch and—darkness. After careful scrutiny of the *Reader's Digest Handyman's Guide,* I realized the problem was with the ballast. Until then I had thought that the word *ballast* was strictly a boating term. My wife saw my confusion and gently suggested I consult our next-door neighbor, a "jack of all trades" kind of man.

I would hear nothing of her counsel. "I can do it. Why, all that needs to be done is to remove a few screws and put a new light in." My layer of blustering bravado required me to ignore directions, advice, and common sense. In a few minutes of unscrewing, pulling, and jiggling, I succeeded in pulling the ballast from its base. A host of connecting wires came with it midst a shower of sparks. The fruit of my effort was a bent light and protruding wires.

Enter now the layer of assertive avoidance. My patient wife waited nearly six weeks before I mounted a second attack on the light. During that time I promised to address the problem, but I put off any action. My goal, I must painfully admit, was to avoid feeling incompetent for bungling an easy job. Avoidance meant safety from the pain of admitting failure. Two comfortable layers: bravado and avoidance, aimed at avoiding exposure and projecting confidence.

The masks I wear may be quite different from yours, but all of us have found effective strategies for protecting ourselves from one another. An encourager must leave the warm hearth of layered security and venture into the sometimes howling winds of rejection and failure without the protection of artificial layers. Then, and then alone, will he know the deep warmth that the cloak of Christ's righteousness brings. With layers on, we depend on our sufficiency; with layers removed, we can trust in His.

If we can face our natural tendency to manipulate others, then we can begin to alter those patterns of speech that lead to manipulation instead of to ministry. We must also acknowledge that we are layered people who find it much easier to relate to others from behind our protective patterns. If we can become aware of those layers, then we can drop them.

As encouragers we must be willing to do the hard work of brutally honest introspection. Otherwise our words will be manipulative, spoken from layers, and destructive. We are to encourage others with words that bring life.

This chapter and the next are concerned with the practical development of communication skills that facilitate life-giving encouragement. What are those skills, and how do we develop them? Once we understand and go to work on overcoming the problems of manipulation and layers, we are ready to learn the actual skills involved in the ministry of encouragement.

THE MINDSET OF AN ENCOURAGER

As we turn our attention to skills and techniques, remember that encouragement cannot be packaged into nicely wrapped boxes of appropriate words. You may recall how unmeaningful it was to hear someone respond, "I'll pray for you," after you had shared a difficult problem. Those words ought to have awesome power to encourage, because prayer is our vital link with the Lord. So why do they sometimes not move us? Because words have power only to the degree that they represent meaningful involvement.

Encouragement requires involvement in other peoples' lives, a sacrificial giving that refuses to consider the cost of the gift. This is unconditional love: a well-worn term, but one that speaks of a deep, dynamic reality. Unconditional love is not a three-step process or a quick pop-psychology-do-it-yourself feeling to be learned after reading a book or attending a seminar. It is learned by living in the power of the resurrected Savior. And that is a lifetime affair. The focus of this book is on *attitude* rather than on *what to say*. So we begin our discussion of techniques of encouragement by looking at the mindset of the encourager.

The Book of Proverbs defines the kind of attitude that must reflect itself in our words. Notice that the power of words depends on the character of the speaker.

> The mouth of the righteous is a fountain of life, but the mouth of the wicked conceals violence (Prov. 10:11).
>
> The tongue of the righteous is as choice silver, but the heart of the wicked is worth little (Prov. 10:20).
>
> There is one who speaks rashly like the thrusts of a sword, but the tongue of the wise brings healing (Prov. 12:18).
>
> A soothing tongue is a tree of life, but perversion in it crushes the spirit (Prov. 15:4).
>
> Death and life are in the power of the tongue, and those who love it will eat its fruit (Prov. 18:21).

The encourager is to be joyfully and responsibly aware of the great potential his words have to heal or destroy. Words are like a sharp blade; each person is responsible to determine whether his words cut like a mugger's knife or a surgeon's scalpel.

An encourager must know the power of his words and use that force to build up his Christian brothers and sisters. He must use his words carefully. From the Book of Proverbs emerge three principles that should guide him as he speaks.

Principle 1: Be Slow to Speak
Proverbs 12:18; 13:3; 17:27-28; 29:20

Researchers have found that human beings can listen at least three times faster than they can talk. This suggests that we can daydream, plan our week's menu, hum a favorite tune, and still "listen" to our neighbor's chatter. If we could hear what others are thinking as we talk to them, it might be disconcerting: "I'll listen long enough to get an idea of what you are saying, then I'll begin to plan my response." That is not listening. Proverbs 18:13 says, "He who gives an answer before he hears, it is folly and shame to him." As encouragers we must be slow to speak so that we can concentrate on what others are saying. Then our words will fit the concerns that the others have expressed.

Principle 2: Be sensitive in your speech

An encourager's response must be well-tuned and suited both to the circumstances and the personality of the one speaking. After preaching at a country church, I received an invitation to dine with a respected but somewhat intimidating deacon and his family. Listening to him expound on the need for an iron hand in ruling the church and the home, I noticed that all of us in the room felt thoroughly threatened by him because he always spoke harshly and seemed to regard everyone else as wrong.

After dinner, the deacon's four-year-old granddaughter was helping the women clear the table when she stumbled. She dropped several pieces of the "Sunday china." I was seized with terror, expecting a verbal guillotine to fall on the child's neck. But to my amazement, the old gentleman quickly reached over to stroke the little girl's hair and soothed her muffled cry. He responded with sensitivity to a frightened child. A harsh word would have turned her into a pool of tears; instead, his timing and touch averted a catastrophe.

The lesson in this incident is that an encourager is sensitive. An encourager asks himself questions like "What words will be most effective in touching this person?" and "What does the situation demand of me to help this person grow in Christ?"

Sensitivity requires real awareness of situations and a basic knowledge of how people typically feel in different circumstances. Before I respond to someone who has failed in a task, I must remind myself that the task is less important than the person. My verbal response must reflect thoughtful concern for the person who has failed. Only then will negative feedback about performance qualify as constructive criticism. If I don't exercise this sensitivity, my comments will be destructive.

Principle 3: Be gentle in your speech
Proverbs 15:1, 4; 26:21

Clanging words are motivated by something other than love. The air is full of such noise. Many words are spoken to demonstrate competency, to exhibit success, to control others, or to enhance a reputation. I remember listening to a family conversation that more closely resembled a volleyball game than good communication. The subject was travel, and each participant took great pleasure in sharing his experiences. For some reason I fell to counting the number of times the subject was bounced back and forth before one person asked another to elaborate on what was just said. I stopped counting at twenty-six. Their words were like slaps at a ball; there was no interest in what the other person was saying. Kind words show involvement and concern. Selfish words clamor for the spotlight; they interrupt rather than facilitate conversation.

Gentle words, it should be said, are not necessarily softly spoken. Rather, they are words *seasoned with grace*. Gentle words may resemble the soft, firm touch of the shepherd's crook guiding the sheep down the safest path. Gentle words may convince us that there is no need to keep our layers on, thereby freeing us to express the concerns that are troubling us or the joys that are filling us. The measure of gentleness is less a matter of tone than of motive.

We recently spent time with friends whom we had not seen for a number of months. During a weeklong sailing trip, we talked at some length about our growth in Christ. We laughed, we were serious, and we enjoyed one another's company. At the end of the week, I realized the time had refreshed my spirit. Words were spoken that caused me to reflect on my relationship with the Lord, on His love for me, and on the high calling of service for Him. Our conversation was filled with mutual love and interest. The words were gentle. Gentle words result in the softening of layers, enabling us to look honestly at ourselves and appreciatively at Christ.

An encourager, therefore, will enter into even superficial conversations with an eye toward speaking gently, aware of the context and the person. He wants his words to break down layers through kind, involved interaction. Every Christian can speak gently. More must do so.

Perhaps the major obstacle to becoming an encourager is the universal and natural appetite for self-satisfaction. Even the most saintly man or woman will fall back into old patterns of self-centered living. It takes real work to speak *slowly, sensitively, and gently.*

RESPONSES THAT INHIBIT ENCOURAGEMENT

As we give attention to these three simple characteristics of encouraging words, it might be helpful to pinpoint a few verbal habits that violate these principles. Often our natural response to situations is to speak quickly, insensitively, and harshly. Consider a few typical patterns of response that interfere with encouragement.

1. Defensive or explanatory words

Picture a husband coming home late from work and finding his family glued to the television set. His wife interrupts her stare for a moment to snap, "About time you're home! Dinner's already cold." His response might be governed by one of several ideas: (1) protect yourself at all costs; (2) the best offense is a good defense; or (3) the loudest word wins. He explains that his boss gave him an armful of work at the last minute, the car wouldn't start, and there was an accident on the bridge. "And every phone booth I passed had someone talking in it, and anyway if I had stopped to call you, it would have just made me later." Why the explanation? His intention is to place his behavior in a better light and to avoid the harassments of an angry wife.　　*motive*

2. Apologies

Another frequent response to someone who shares a complaint with you is an apology.

"George, I wish you had called before you went to the store."

"I'm sorry, honey."

Quick apologies cut off conversation and block an opportunity for the problem to be expressed and understood.

3. Attack/Cutting Remarks

Humor in current times is often sarcastic, derisive, and critical. The satire and insolent humor of popular comedians have left their mark on the conversational style of many Christians. One husband whom I counseled remarked to his wife as he walked in the door one evening, "Well, what has Chef Boyardee cooked up for us tonight?. . .No kidding, you made it yourself? Will miracles never cease?"

Church groups can become competitive societies that thrive on matching cutting remark for cutting remark. "Hey, how's the welfare office?" says one to a friend who has lost a job. Or "How's the diet coming? Got some of that fat off yet?" says another to an overweight member of the fellowship. Cruel jesting hurts.

4. Corrections

Another violation of encouragement involves telling someone that he is not feeling what he claims to feel. A husband remarks, "I'm so discouraged; I don't know how I am going to make it."

His wife responds, "Honey, you don't feel that bad; everything is going to work out fine." As her husband storms off unencouraged, she wonders why her words did not help. She doesn't realize that feelings must first be accepted. The thoughts and behaviors accompanying the emotions may later require correction; often they do. But emotions must be accepted as they are.

5. Quick advice

When someone shares a problem, he wants to be understood before listening to solutions. Many men have wondered why their wives responded to helpful advice by becoming indignant or hurt. "All I wanted to do was help." We often give advice without first understanding the problem.

When my wife was preparing for her first public talk to a women's group, she was unnerved and anxious. I helpfully suggested that she develop a quick outline. I then shared a few appropriate Scriptures and warmly kissed her on the cheek. She did not relax. As a matter of fact, she tightened more. Now she worried that I would be critical if she stayed nervous. Quick advice missed the real problem.

Advice—even sound advice—can be heard as negative. When a friend suggests that we pull into a gas station for directions after hours of aimless wandering, we are rarely spurred on to love and good deeds. The message we hear is: "You dummy, why don't you find someone who can get us out of our mess!"

These five strategies for discouragement are only some of the many ways it is possible to reject a person who shares a feeling. We must attend to all violations of the principles of slow, sensitive, and gentle speech.

In the next chapter, we will look more closely at specific verbal techniques that can transform ordinary conversation into moments of profound encouragement.

SUMMARY

To become an encourager, we must first identify our manipulative layers and determine to pursue the goal of ministry.

Secondly, we must discipline ourselves to speak slowly, to be sensitive to the needs and problems of the person with whom we are speaking, and to speak gently with the purpose of reducing fear.

Then we must avoid responding to people in ways that communicate rejection of what they are sharing. We must not defend, apologize, attack, correct, or offer quick advice.

13
Techniques of Encouragement: II

Understanding what it means to offer rich, meaningful encouragement is no simple matter. A friend who participated in one of our encouragement seminars remarked, "I expected encouragement to be learned quickly in three easy steps. But instead of learning a few formulas, you've got me asking some hard questions about what's going on in others and even harder questions about what's going on in me."

My friend got the point. Encouragement, as we understand it, is more than acquiring a new set of skills. It is the fruit of a self-examined heart and a compassionate, discerning sensitivity to the needs of others. "For the mouth speaks out of that which fills the heart" (Matt. 12:34). Humble, loving hearts produce encouraging words. Hearts insensitive to their own deceitfulness, unbroken and proud, will never produce deeply encouraging words no matter how smooth and appropriate their words may be.

But encouragement is more than an attitude. It does involve certain skills. Because words are a prime form of communication, we need to concern ourselves with choosing words that properly convey our hearts' intent. This chapter focuses on a few verbal strategies which, when motivated by a right heart, will be encouraging.

Consider a simple situation that resulted in my being on the receiving end of both encouragement and discouragement. As you read the interchange, ask what was encouraging or discouraging about each moment.

My wife and I had drooled over a planned sailing vacation for more than a year. Sacrificing a few pleasures and hoarding our pennies helped us to afford a week on the west coast of Florida at a sailing school. A week of sheer joy—rich time together, fun on the water, and rejoicing in God's blessings—rewarded our long anticipation.

When the week was over, we returned to the wintry climate of our northern home. Moving quickly from tropical paradise to snow-covered streets proved to be a major culture shock. I was mature enough to accept the loss of paradise without slipping into a sulk or depression, but I did feel a grudging reluctance as I dragged myself back to work bundled up in overcoat and gloves. An appeal to "rejoice evermore" or to "fight the good fight" would not have moved me at that moment. I was mildly down.

Eavesdrop on two conversations that took place shortly after my return home:

Fred: "Looks like you got some sun."

Dan: "Becky and I just spent a week in Florida. Great weather. We went sailing for a week."

Fred: "Jet set life, huh? Must be doing better than most of us. Too bad the tan won't last up here." (Fred then laughed a decidedly sarcastic laugh.)

Dan: "I know, but it was worth it just to get away, relax, and spend time together. It's hard though to get back to the grind of. . . ."

Fred: "Grind! At least you got away! Well, look, we better figure out when we can get together to work on that project that's due. . ."

Before the conversation I was mildly discouraged. Afterward I was moderately discouraged—less inclined to return to my responsibilities, more affected by the realities of a sometimes unpleasant life. Why? Fred is a friend of mine. He is not typically unkind toward me. Nor did he seem especially vindictive or angry during our interchange. Yet his words were discouraging.

Fred was wrapped up in his world, unconcerned about the effect of his words on me, insensitive to what I was feeling. He never acknowledged my emotions; he battered them. Rather than express understanding, he scorned my sluggishness. He failed to give me a perspective to help me carry on; instead he reminded me of my duties.

Listen to the other conversation:

Jane: "Hi, Dan! Hey, good tan! When did you get back?"

Dan: "Just two days ago."

Jane: "How was it—a good time?"

Dan: "It was great! Just what Becky and I needed to unwind. Makes it hard to come back though. After eighty-degree days, below zero is hard to take."

Jane: "I'll bet! Probably hard to believe you were even there. How's Becky taking her reentry to the real world?"

Dan: "Better than me, I think. Her schedule up here is tough, but a little more flexible than mine. I feel the contrast between having nothing to do for a week and having to meet time demands again."

Jane: "So you're the struggling one now."

Dan: "I'm not proud of it, but I am."

Jane: "Your school and work schedule is really pretty demanding of your time, isn't it?"

Dan: "Becky and I had so much undisturbed time just to be together—and up here I'm lucky if I get any quality time with her at all. I'm afraid our commitments to other things might damage some of the closeness we feel with each other."

Jane: "So it's not just missing warm weather and sailing that's getting you."

Dan: "I guess not. Maybe the trip helped me realize that my priorities were out of line, and now I'm afraid I'll get them fouled up again."

The contrast between the first and second conversations is dramatic, but not overdone. They happened just that way. Jane made an effort to understand me. She esteemed another's concerns greater than her own. She responded to *my* needs rather than to hers. Her encouraging words prompted me to evaluate what my struggles really were. With a better grip on my real problem clarifying the challenge that lay before me, I felt a renewed sense of commitment to keep my life in order. Jane had stirred me to love and good deeds.

How did Jane do it? Assuming the rightness of her motives (speaking from her love to my fear), what did she do that encouraged me?

The answer to the question lies in two concepts that are the focus of this chapter. People who encourage (1) attend to their own *nonverbal messages,* and (2) they develop skills in *four verbal techniques.*

NONVERBAL MESSAGES

Have you ever talked with someone who stares at the wall behind you while you speak? How about the person who shuffles papers at his desk while you pour out your heart, or the one who picks his fingernails or twirls his ring while you tell him about your child's sickness? Nonverbal behaviors like these communicate a clear message: "I'm not especially interested in what you're saying. Would you please hurry up and finish?"

The written version of the conversation between Jane and me cannot, of course, demonstrate her nonverbal messages, but I noticed that she was behaving in a way that reflected involvement with me. Perhaps five simple suggestions adequately summarize what Jane communicated nonverbally and what other people can do to encourage without words.

1. Squarely face the other person.

Jane stood facing me directly. Standing sideways to someone says, "You're not the center of my attention."

2. Openly face the other person.

Tightly crossed arms and legs communicate distance and inhibit the development of closeness. I remember an angry wife in counseling whose arms went from tensely locked across her stomach to comfortably limp on the chair as she learned to accept her husband.

3. Lean forward.

Position yourself toward the other. A slight lean of the body or head communicates attentive interest.

4. Eye contact.

Your eye contact should avoid the one extreme of a merciless stare and the opposite extreme of looking at everything but the other's eyes. Some researchers indicate that length of eye contact is a pretty good measure of intimacy in a relationship. A good rule of thumb is that *speakers* may break uncomfortable eye contact; *listeners* should maintain fairly steady eye contact.

5. Relax.

Although relaxing is easier said than done and clearly something that cannot be forced, encouragers need to consciously relax as they chat. Be natural and comfortable. Don't mimic someone you admire by sitting the way he sits.

These five principles might be easily remembered with the simple acronym SOLER: [1]

S: Squarely face
O: Openly face
L: Lean forward
E: Eye contact
R: Relax

A further thought on developing a good nonverbal style is to invite feedback from friends. Most of us are not aware of what we do when we speak. We might ask our spouse or a close friend to evaluate us in light of SOLER. We can solicit comments on habits that others find distracting or annoying.

FOUR VERBAL SKILLS

Encouragers should be aware of four skills or techniques that will not *replace* good motives but may help to *express* them properly.

1. Reflection

People are naturally forgetful. Sometimes we forget what we wanted to remember ("Where did I leave the car keys?"). At other times we forget what we don't want to remember ("I don't know what she said to me"). The latter involves selective inattention, a desire to forget something unpleasant.

Most of us are skilled in noticing flaws in another but overlooking faults in ourselves. Husbands and wives waste a great deal of counseling time (if counselors let them) rehearsing in angry detail what their spouses have done. Their memory functions quite well in recalling the other's irritating behavior.

So often, however, the memory stumbles in coming up with one's own contribution to a dilemma. The attention simply is not there. It is natural to be selectively inattentive to what we do wrong, to remain unaware of our real feelings and motives.

---

[1]For a fuller discussion of SOLER, see Gerard Egan, *The Skilled Helper;* 2nd edition (Monterey, Calif.: Brooks/Cole Publishing Company, 1982).

An encourager sometimes needs to serve as a mirror, reflecting back to the speaker what he is really feeling, doing, and pursuing. Problems will be dealt with only when they are acknowledged. Reflection uncovers problems which require attention but which our selective memory system (a fancy label for part of our sinful nature) tends to ignore.

Two examples will illustrate how reflection mirrors for the speaker a present reality that he is neglecting.

John: "Sue is never on time. We haven't been to church on time for years, or anyplace else for that matter!"

Bill: "You are really ticked off at her. Sounds like her habits are getting you upset."

Notice that the focus changes from Sue's lateness to John's upset. The shift is crucial. John cannot directly do a thing about his wife's tardy ways, but he can deal with his own attitudes. Encouragement by reflection has highlighted a matter that calls for increased love and good works.

Bob: "School is such a long haul. Only three years to go and I graduate. Seems forever and then what?"

Joan: "Sounds like you're struggling with the purpose of all this hard work."

Again, the focus moves away from the tediousness of school (an unchangeable reality) toward questions about purpose, which through prayer and counsel can be answered. Reflection does exactly what the word implies: it reflects back to the speaker the real problem that requires attention.

2. Clarification

Perhaps the greatest obstacle to effective communication is our tendency to think we know what another person is saying when we don't. Language is like a multifaceted jewel: just as the colors change when the gem is turned in light, so new shades of meaning become apparent every time we consider someone's words from another angle.

The skill of clarification is required to determine whether we have studied the other's words from enough angles to arrive at a good picture of what was meant. The actual technique is as embarrassingly simple as it is underused. All that is required is to ask what the speaker meant, or to repeat back what you think he meant, and to ask if you've got the meaning. The point is, don't assume; check it out.

> Tony: "This tax return is a mess. It's driving me crazy."
> Sally: "What's the problem, honey?"

Sally is clarifying Tony's message. To do so invites further interaction. If Sally wanted to slam the door on more conversation, she could have replaced her clarifying question with a comment like "You've put it off till April—should've gotten to it before this," or something more gentle like "I'm sure you can handle it."

Clarification encourages the speaker to state more clearly what is happening inside, where it counts. Once a problem is keenly understood, remedies are more easily recognized. Remember that the final aim of encouragement is to move people along in their walk with Christ. To clarify a problem makes it more susceptible to biblical resolution.

3. Exploring

Reflection and clarification open conversational doors, but sometimes the people we want to encourage make a polite retreat from the door we've opened. At other times they walk through by sharing a bit more of what they feel or think.

When someone willingly discusses more of what is happening, the encourager can quietly seize the opportunity by exploring in more detail the issues that may need biblical attention. Open-ended questions rather than yes-no questions can often move the exploration forward. For example, the inquiry "Tell me how you felt when that happened" is more probing than "Were you really mad?"

Let's return to an earlier example:

> John: "Sue is never on time. We haven't been to church on time for a year, or anyplace else for that matter!"
> Bill: "You are really ticked off at her. Sounds like her habits are getting you really upset." (*Reflection*)
> John: "Yes, they really are. I really get mad sometimes."
> Bill: "How do you let her know you're mad? What do you do?" (*Clarification*)
> John: "Oh, I never hit her, if that's what you're thinking. I guess I just clam up, maybe once in a while blow up."
> Bill: "What happens when you back away or yell at her? I

wonder if she understands why you're upset?" (*Explora-tion*)

Now Bill is probing. He is inviting John to consider more fully the effects of his behavior on Sue. John walked through Bill's open door by admitting how he handles his anger. The scene is set for a more detailed discussion of John's motives and behavior that may lead to conviction, repentance, and remedy.

Exploring is central to the encouragement process. Many Christians today have lost the capacity for spiritual self-examina-tion. *Why* we do what we do as well as *what* we actually do should be pressing concerns for every Christian. Only when the wrong motives beneath irresponsible behavior are brought to light can they be corrected. Exploring is an effort to further uncover hidden problems that are hindering spiritual growth.

4. Intimate interaction

By this time—after reflecting, clarifying, and exploring—the conversation may have become uncomfortable. The person we are seeking to encourage may feel naked and ashamed and, like Adam, look for the nearest hiding place.

Encouragers, too, may feel awkward when things progress to personal matters. Both parties may tacitly agree to retreat to a more comfortable distance and politely replace their layers: "Oh, by the way, did you catch the ballgame on TV last night?" or "Well, I guess struggles are part of life. It'll sure be fun to get to heaven. I'm ready."

When someone has responded to your reflection, when he has willingly clarified what he really meant, when he has let you probe a little more deeply into a painful situation, then it is time to explicitly deal with the intimacy that is developing. The opportu-nity for rich encouragement should not be missed. Be courageous. Put into words what is happening.

> "John, we're talking about pretty personal matters. What you've brought up sounds like it may be really important to think through. I don't have a bunch of answers which I'm waiting to dump on you, but I'd sure like to keep talking about your problems with Sue. I really don't want to push my way into your personal life, but I do enjoy talking things through with you."

The interaction has now reached beneath the layers to the core. Loving and attentive listening, carefully offered advice, patient acceptance, and firm but tender rebuke are all available now to the encourager as he speaks from his love to the other's fear.

The next stage of the helping process involves discerning core problems and offering biblical remedies that require skills beyond encouragement. The next chapter focuses on deeper levels of counseling that deal with problems needing more than encouragement.

SUMMARY

Nonverbal messages must consistently and clearly express involvement. The SOLER acronym is helpful for sending positive nonverbal messages:

Squarely face
Openly face
Lean forward
Eye contact
Relax

Verbal techniques should open doors to deeper levels of hearing until the person's real thoughts and motives are clearly exposed in the context of a noncritical relationship. This defines encouragement: exposure without rejection. There are four important techniques to be mastered in this regard: Reflection, Clarification, Exploring, and Intimate Interaction.

14
The Local Church: A Restoring Community

Restoring some disfigured thing to its original condition is an activity that invariably yields a satisfying sense of fulfillment. Tasks such as refinishing a dull, scratched chair, washing an especially dirty car, or straightening up a messy garage are simple examples of restoration efforts that bring a measure of joy. The joy, it should be noted, lies less in the *work* of restoration than in the *awareness of participation* in the project. The work itself may be frustrating, tedious, and difficult. But the fulfillment of looking at something restored from bad to good condition, knowing that you had a part in the restoration, is worth the labor.

The church is meant to be vitally involved in a restoration process, helping men and women toward higher levels of spiritual maturity and Christlikeness. But the work is hard. Sin has made such an utter wreck of our lives that the task of restoration is very difficult. People need to be thoroughly restored, inside and out. No part of the human personality has been left untouched by sin's corrupting mark. Motives, emotions, thoughts, choices, behavior, beliefs, aspirations—every facet of human life is stained by sin.

Jesus Christ came to restore His fallen creation to its original splendor. And He does His work completely. Churches that promote a success mentality and focus on building up self-esteem through positive thinking may be encouraging merely an appearance of togetherness: people look good, they smile, they attend church, and they may stay married. But this is not enough. God wants people who are absolutely committed to Him, who consider it their main privilege and responsibility to worship Him. And who, with the overflowing fulness that comes from knowing God, want to live lives of joyful service for Him.

This is the work of restoration, to help people who are essentially self-centered, unbelieving, and fearful to become thoroughly Christ-centered, trusting, and bold. God has commissioned the family and the church to be His primary agents of restoration. Husbands and wives are to proclaim the Christ-church relationship in their style of relating—husbands leading with love and strength, and wives submitting with trust and contentment. Parents are to teach their children the truth of God and to discipline them for violating that truth and, above all, to love them no matter what. Children are to recognize authority and to learn the benefits and joys of willful obedience to authority. These are the guidelines for the work of restoration in the family.

But how about the church? How are local assemblies of believers to approach the task of restoring Christlike character? How are they to foster growth in wisdom, moral conviction, and resolute determination to do what is right?

In this closing chapter I want to sketch a plan—not a tested and proven formula—for developing our churches into effective restoring communities, where the reality of relationship with God is felt with steady, life-changing impact.

The model I present can work only in churches that are already moving in the right direction. Local churches must emphasize (1) the value and importance of worship, (2) the teaching of the Word of God, (3) the radical nature of discipleship, and (4) the importance and uniqueness of Christian fellowship. Too many churches elevate *service for God* above *worship of God.* The result is shallow though extensive service. Some churches replace teaching the Word with Bible-related discussions designed to interest, inspire, and challenge. Instruction in discipleship is sometimes reduced to a list of approved and disapproved activities with no concern for the cost of absolute surrender. Fellowship too often is a Christian-sounding label attached to conversations that could just as easily be shared by children of darkness.

Churches must begin with clear recognition of the need for worship, teaching, discipleship, and fellowship. Such an emphasis can lead naturally into evangelism and the exercise of spiritual gifts. Efforts to develop evangelism programs and to encourage ministry according to gifts will likely not reach their richest potential without a prior insistence on worship, teaching discipleship, and fellowship. With that insistence, evangelism will be fervent and ministry will be effective.

It is into this kind of church—already involved effectively in the restoration of people—that I want to introduce the model. My desire is to give suggestions that can help the church to become an even more effective restoring community. The model I am presenting offers a strategy for incorporating the ministry of counseling into the natural life of the local church.

It is important, in my view, that counseling be regarded as part of the church's *natural* service. Hiring a professionally trained Christian counselor and providing him with office space in the church building or in church-owned property is *not* what I mean by "counseling in the local church body." Much good, I suppose, can be accomplished if a truly biblical counselor is employed by a church, but to think that hiring a professional handles the counseling needs in a church is a serious mistake.

Counseling is not a profession akin to dentistry or medicine. It must *not* be seen as an optional, separate, external appendage to the church program. The ministry of counseling should rather be regarded as an essential (not necessarily central) part of the mainstream of church life. We must stop thinking of counseling as a professional activity that belongs to psychologists and psychiatrists and begin to realize that the work of counseling represents one more means through which Christians can grow and unbelievers can hear the gospel.

If, as I maintain, counseling is basically the skillful application of biblical truth to individual lives, then obviously it belongs to the church. My desire to see counseling in the church does *not* reflect a desire to shift the focus of church life from worship, teaching, discipleship, and fellowship. Churches that shift their focus from these essentials to a counseling ministry (sharing groups, individual sessions, and the like) can easily become a sort of Neurotics Anonymous Association.

However, churches that are strong in the basics but neglect the resources of counseling in ministering to individual needs can become sterile and academic, or perhaps theologically top-heavy to the point where the *relevance* of truth to human need is obscured.

Church leadership, therefore, needs to make sure that (1) the congregation is involved in worship, Bible learning, concern for personal spiritual growth, and fellowship; (2) resources and opportunities exist for developing evangelistic efforts and for using the gifts in the body; and (3) the potential of a counseling ministry is carefully studied. My desire is to introduce counseling into the natural life of the local church for the purpose of helping the church become a more effective restoring community. How can it be done? Consider a three-level model.

LEVEL I COUNSELING: ENCOURAGEMENT

Christians who are worshiping God, studying the Bible, discipling or being discipled, and enjoying fellowship with one another can develop an effective ministry of encouragement. Encouragement is not the responsibility of a gifted few; it is the privilege of every believer. Every Christian can and should be an encourager.

Many problems that have potential to become serious difficulties (such as divorce, marital infidelity, or compromise with the world) can sometimes be resolved at early stages through the caring involvement of an encouraging person. Conflicts that apparently require extensive individual counseling might have never become so serious in many cases if meaningful encouragement had occurred. If church leaders desire to build a counseling ministry, they should not think first of all in terms of making a handful of counselors available to the congregation. Rather, they should alert the members to what they can do through the ministry of encouragement and then train them to do it.

Suppose the entire church were to learn how to spot layers, open doors, and speak in ways that reduce others' fears. The pastor could offer an annual series of sermons on the "one another" commands of the New Testament. Occasional Saturday morning workshops or Sunday evening services could be devoted to demonstrating conversations that open doors and reduce fear. Small-group Bible studies provide a natural opportunity to talk about encouragement and to share conversations that group members have found encouraging.

This book and others dealing with the same theme could be used as a study guide for Sunday School classes or study groups.[1] A series of thirteen half-hour lectures dealing with the concepts in

---

[1]Examples are *The People Helper Growthbook* by Gary Collins (Vision House, 1976) and *How to Help a Friend* by Paul Welter (Tyndale, 1978).

this book have been recorded on videotape and are available for rental.[2] People in the church with a special interest in the ministry of encouragement could develop other materials and strategies for helping Christians to encourage one another effectively.

Churches should not only emphasize the importance and how-to's of encouragement, but also provide opportunities for light, happy fellowship that can develop warm feelings of belonging. The trend in too many churches is toward sharing times, unburdening sessions, and gut-wrenching group confessions and away from hayrides, potluck dinners, and skit nights. We need to create an atmosphere in which people can simply have wholesome fun and not make every Christian gathering into a "heavy" occasion.

If a church could capture the vision of becoming an encouraging community and then equip its people to involve themselves in each others' lives for the purpose of encouragement, then perhaps the truth of God's Word would find more fertile soil in which to take root.

Nevertheless, a word of caution is in order. A great danger is that a church will catch the vision and then feel an enthusiasm that creates unrealistic expectations. The unhappy fact is that some people will not even attempt to encourage. Others will become pests, looking for any crack in the door through which they can slip their meddlesome feet. Some will sincerely speak words designed to encourage but will mishandle problems in their own lives. Eventually their zeal for encouragement will disappear.

A certain number will really catch on. The development of encouragement in the body may be a slow and barely visible process. But faithfulness in well-doing even when fatigue sets in will be rewarded. The Christian life is not a short sprint on a fast track; it is a marathon race over rough terrain. An initial burst of speed ("Let's have an encouragement seminar!") is less important to success than a steady, sustained pace. We must not lose heart in our efforts to build encouragement into the life of our churches.

LEVEL II COUNSELING: EXHORTATION

If counseling is to realize its potential as a ministry in the body, we must go beyond counseling-by-encouragement. Encour-

---

[2] Information is available through Columbia Bible College, P.O. Box 3122, Columbia, South Carolina 29230-3122, (803) 754-4100.

agement is a necessary beginning, but it is hardly a comprehensive and sufficient emphasis. More is required.

A handful of people (perhaps one for every seventy-five to one hundred church members) need to learn more specific strategies for assisting people with definite problems. Married couples with communication difficulties or sexual tensions, parents who are confused about handling their children, young people contemplating marriage, middle-aged men who become depressed with no apparent cause are all examples of people who could profit from direct biblical counsel about resolving these problems.

Perhaps a small group of Christians who have shown special interest in encouragement could be invited to meet together to discuss their people-helping efforts. As they interact about their experiences, the discussion could be directed toward enlarging their vision for working with troubled persons. Hypothetical and real cases could be evaluated. What is behind the problem? What does the Bible say about it? What solutions can be applied? The group could roleplay conversations between the person with a problem and the counselor in order to think through verbal strategies for applying biblical solutions.

It is generally a mistake to select ten people, put them through a training program, and then present them as counselors available to the congregation. A wiser course is to continue emphasizing encouragement, to spend extra time with those who demonstrate facility in encouraging people, to expose them to further training, and then to let them develop their own counseling ministries through the natural opportunities of everyday interaction. After a year or two, the ones whom God has uniquely gifted for a ministry in counseling will have risen to the surface. If at that time it seems advantageous to increase the visibility of these counselors who have proven themselves, then a more formal counseling ministry could be established.

An increasing amount of literature and training seminars that can provide substantial help are available for those who desire to become Level II counselors. Dr. Jay Adams has written a great deal of helpful material and offers both live and taped seminars. A growing number of churches have used the texts I have written as a framework for training programs.[3]   The Institute of Biblical Counseling (IBC) offers a thirty-five-hour seminar in various

---

[3]*Basic Principles of Biblical Counseling* (Zondervan, 1975) and *Effective Biblical Counseling* (Zondervan, 1977).

locations around the country specifically designed to train Level II counselors.[4]

This training is adequate to equip people to discern key problems behind complaints and to present practical and workable biblical remedies. Another caution is in order. For every ten people who take on the ministry of Level II counseling, six or seven will either discontinue or prove unsuited for the task. It is crucial to work closely with those who persevere and to stay alert for others who may be uniquely capable of such a ministry.

Level II counselors must see their work not necessarily as their *exclusive* ministry but certainly as their *priority* ministry. Efforts to bring biblical truth to bear on someone's specific problems will often prove frustrating. But the value of counseling must not be measured in terms of percentages of those who improve; instead it must be seen in terms of the opportunity to meaningfully communicate biblical insights and perspectives to hurting people. The ministry, however discouraging at times, must be regarded as a committed priority.

LEVEL III COUNSELING: ENLIGHTENMENT

There is an obvious snag in the proposal as stated. Perhaps we can agree that training in Level I and Level II counseling is desirable and potentially most valuable. But who will provide the training? Seminars, books, and taped courses are good teaching aids, but an available, live teacher is still needed.

Most pastors are already overburdened with responsibilities and cannot give the time necessary for the program to flourish. And it must be recognized that too few pastors have the counseling expertise to train others effectively.

Every congregation needs someone (or at least access to someone) who regards counseling as a major vocation and who is equipped by education and experience to train others in Levels I and II counseling. This person should also be available to handle the more complicated personal tangles that do not respond to either encouragement or exhortation. He needs the discernment and wisdom to uncover the cherished but wrong ideas that fearful people hold about how their fears can be relieved. His work will go beyond *encouragement* and *exhortation* to include *enlightenment*. Call this person a Level III counselor.

[4]Information is available by writing to IBC, 100 Fifth Street, Winona Lake, Indiana 46590.

Training opportunities for Level III counseling exist in a variety of Christian schools. Several seminaries offer master's level work in counseling. In some instances, however, the training program insists that pastoral counseling is for lighter problems and that more serious problems require psychotherapy. In my terms, pastoral counseling is roughly equivalent to Level II counseling. Level III counseling, as I conceive it, is meant to *replace* nonmedical psychotherapy.

In the conviction that master's level intensive training is sufficient to produce a Level III counselor, a Master of Arts in Biblical Counseling is offered through Grace Theological Seminary in Winona Lake, Indiana. It is our intention to train people that can assume the responsibilities of Level III counseling. These responsibilities include—

— providing overall direction, both conceptual and administrative, for a local church counseling ministry;
— organizing and leading workshops and classes on Level I counseling (Encouragement);
— training selected people in Level II counseling (Exhortation);
— providing supervision for Level II counselors;
— assuming counseling responsibility for more difficult cases.

The model then suggests three levels of counseling: (1) encouraging people by speaking sensitively to their hidden fears; (2) exhorting people by specifying biblical solutions to their problems in living; (3) enlightening people to understand why their lives are disordered and how they can effect a deep change in their approach to life.

The model is easy to sketch but hard to implement. Problems can arise in many areas. It is difficult to keep people encouraged to encourage and to train and supervise Level II counselors properly. Finding a Level III counselor who can teach, organize, administer, and counsel can also be problematic. Developing a counseling ministry that is complementary and not competitive with other church activities is a primary concern, along with articulating for the church leadership a clear position on what defines biblical counseling. These and other obstacles stand squarely in the way of developing counseling as a meaningful ministry in the church; but they must be hurdled.

A good place to start is with a focus on encouragement. People are hurting; fear is lodged in deep places. We pretend, we hide, we wear masks, we arrange our layers snugly around us, and we sacrifice vitality in fellowship. Our distance from each other protects us from hurt, but it also blocks out encouragement.

Only love can deal with fear. And the love that alone can thoroughly calm our fears is the perfect love of God. When love penetrates our layers, when we realize the thrilling reality of unconditional acceptance through Christ's blood, our fear gives way to desire—a desire to follow the Lord.

Although God alone loves perfectly, we can share in the ministry of love. Our words can have great power in people's lives if we—

— make it our goal to minister to others;
— trust the Lord with our hurts and fears;
— express only those emotions that in no way violate our commitment to love;
— listen sincerely to what people say;
— respond to people by opening doors to further sharing;
— learn to speak words that facilitate other people's awareness of their security and significance in Christ.

The sum of the matter is that we are to accept others as God for Christ's sake has accepted us. That is Level I counseling, the ministry of encouragement, a good place to begin in our efforts to strengthen our churches as restoring communities.

"Consider how to stimulate one another to love and good deeds; not forsaking the assembling of yourselves together,. . .but encouraging one another; and all the more, as you see the day drawing near" (Heb. 10:24–25).

IBC Seminars
INSTITUTE OF BIBLICAL COUNSELING

The Institute of Biblical Counseling is a ministry dedicated to equipping Christians to counsel through the community of God's people. IBC offers:

- Intensive one-week counseling seminars around the nation (Level II Seminars).
- Audio cassettes by Dr. Lawrence J. Crabb, Jr.
- Video courses on **Counseling by Encouragement** (Level I Seminar) and **God's Design for Marriage.**
- Supervision Seminars (for graduates of Level II Seminar).
- M.A. in Biblical Counseling (Level III). Available through Grace Theological Seminary, Winona Lake, Indiana 46590.

Counseling Seminar
This week-long course is designed to assist the layman, pastors, and professional counselors to better understand a biblical view of people, their problems, and the solutions available in Christ.

Supervision Seminar
In a one-week course, with limited enrollment (4-8 people), intensive supervision in developing counseling skills is offered.

Advanced Counseling Seminar (Level II)
For those who have completed the counseling seminars, a one-week advanced course is offered which expands the material presented in the first course and covers topics not previously addressed.

YES!
I am interested in additional IBC information on: ☐ **Counseling Seminar** (Level I)
☐ **Supervision Seminar** (Level II)
☐ **Advanced Counseling Seminar** (Level III)

Name _____

Address _____

City/State/Zip _____

Send to: **Institute of Biblical Counseling
200 Seminary Drive
Winona Lake, IN 46590
219-269-6741**